Spiritual Sight
The Manual

Melvin L. Morse, M.D.

And

Isabelle A. Chauffeton Saavedra

Copyright © 2014 Melvin L. Morse M.D. & Isabelle Chauffeton Saavedra

All rights reserved.

ISBN: 0692340580
ISBN-13: 978-0692340585

DEDICATION

To the Universe(s): Thank you!

CONTENTS

1	Spiritual Sight - The Manual	Pg 1
2	Definitions	Pg 4
3	Spiritual Sight	Pg 7
4	How does Spiritual Sight work?	Pg 10
5	How do we process information from the remote site?	Pg 16
6	How do we receive perceptions of a remote site?	Pg 22
7	What is the role of the monitor?	Pg 34
8	Common pitfalls of the process	Pg 40
9	Applications for spiritual healing	Pg 46
10	The spiritual sight protocol	Pg 49
11	Mental discipline is required	Pg 54
12	Spiritual Sight: A spiritual tuning fork	Pg 58
13	The stages of Spiritual Sight	Pg 61
14	The remote site address: Spiritual Sight involves asking God a very specific question	Pg 64
15	Brief overview of the four stages of Spiritual Sight	Pg 67
16	Specific descriptions of each of the stages of Spiritual Sight	Pg 72
17	Stage 1: Preparing the mind	Pg 73
18	Stage 2: First contact	Pg 87

19	Stage 3: Creating a virtual reality	Pg 107
20	The emotional reaction to the site	Pg 133
21	Stage 4: Site contact	Pg 136
22	Session summary	Pg 148
23	Feedback	Pg 151
24	Spiritual Sight, why?	Pg 153
26	About the Authors	Pg 155

SPIRITUAL SIGHT – THE MANUAL

Melvin L. Morse, M.D. and Isabelle Chauffeton Saavedra

"I want to know how God created this world. I am not interested in this or that phenomenon, in the spectrum of this or that element. I want to know God's thoughts, the rest are details."

-- Albert Einstein

Spiritual Sight is a natural ability to access information about a place with or without living beings in it that is not available to the ordinary senses. This innate ability of human beings validates scientific theories that we live in an information-based interconnected energetic universe. The Spiritual Sight protocol echoes a basic spiritual wisdom found in Vedic scripture, Buddhist teachings and in contemporary Christian thought. Both ancient cultural wisdom and modern evolutionary Gaia theory conceptualize all life on earth as being one conscious evolving creative organism. Each one of us is part of a greater consciousness. As such, each one of us has direct access to the creator God and a universal source of knowledge. Spiritual Sight demonstrates this access in an unmistakable fashion that can be life affirming and transformational.

"Intuition is really a sudden immersion of the soul into the universal current of life, where the histories of all people are connected, and we are able to know everything, because it's all written there."

-- Paulo Coelho in "The Alchemist"

Spiritual Sight is a spiritual exercise done with two people working together, one as viewer and the other as the monitor.

It is a controlled form of intuition. The viewer directly accesses specific information from the remote site. The monitor serves as mission control, performing the left brain functions of organizing and documenting the flow of information. The monitor assists the viewer in adhering to the Spiritual Sight protocol. After a session, the team is shown photographs of the remote site to provide immediate direct feedback on the session.

Melvin L. Morse, M.D. and Isabelle Chauffeton Saavedra

Definitions

"God", for this Manual, is defined as the all-knowing Generator of Diversity, an all-inclusive definition, which applies to the major religions and other cultural definitions of God such as Quantum Consciousness.

"Left Brain" is a neuroscience-based metaphor for the executive, ego-based, and language functions of the mind-brain unit. Many of these are based in the left side of the brain.

"Right Brain" is a neuroscientific metaphor for the separate non-verbal consciousness associated with sensory, musical and intuitive human functions. Many of these functions are right brain based.

"The Mind-Brain" is the term many neuroscientists use to describe the complex interrelated relationships between the physical brain and the mind. Clearly a properly functioning brain is needed for the "manifestation of" psychological perception of thoughts, personal identity, memories, emotions and individual consciousness. It is now known, however, that thoughts and experiences can change the physical structure of the brain. The mind and brain are considered by many neuroscientists to be a single functioning unit, a "mind-brain". We talk about manifestation of perceptions and not perceptions directly, because in the case of comatose people, disabled people, people with dementia or Alzheimer, it seems that their unfiltered (by the mind-brain) Consciousness conveys to people trained in Spiritual Sight like us, that they are fully aware of who and where they are, only their mind-brain cannot manifest it; Also in the case of people who have experienced an NDE (Near Death Experience), their mind-brain is not fully functional or even not functional at all at the time of their NDE but they are able to perceive thoughts, personal identity, memories, emotions and individual consciousness while experiencing their NDE. They then MANIFEST these perceptions when they recover brain functions.

Spiritual Sight

The long-awaited reunion of science and spirituality is at hand. Our ability to reach into the mind of God and return with otherwise verifiable information demonstrates that we are all connected to one greater consciousness. Mystic yogic traditions teach that learning the relationship of individual consciousness to the infinite consciousness is the one fundamental requirement of life and the aim of Yoga. The New Testament states "with all wisdom and understanding, God made known to us the mystery of His will to bring unity to all things in heaven and on earth (Ephesians 1:8-10). The Japanese spiritual practice of Sukyo Mahikari similarly teaches that we all individually share consciousness with a creator God.

Practitioners of Sukyo Mahikari work in teams of two people to access God's light energy. This light energy embodies God's infinite knowledge and unconditional love. Anticipating recent advances in quantum physics, Sukyo Mahikari teaches that the realm of ultimate reality is a realm of ultra-infinitesimal spiritual particles. These are but a few examples of this mystical concept held by most of the major religions.

This same principle that we are part of a universal unity of reality is now part of modern scientific theories. Evolutionary biologists accept the concept of Gaia, the theory that man is part of a greater single living organism that consists of all life on earth. Gaia could not survive without light energy. The ultimate source of life is sunlight, which bacteria and plants convert into food for the rest of living organisms.

Theoretical physicists describe reality as consisting of infinitely small subatomic vibrating strings. Long intertwined vibrating strings clump together to form the basic building blocks of material reality, neutrons, electrons, and protons.

These in turn form the basis of atoms and molecules. All of material reality is thought to be linked together and entangled by the event called "The Big Bang." Many theoretical physicists consider material reality to be a self-organizing creative pulsating energetic field with no clear division between living and non-living systems.

For example, Paul Davies, Professor of Mathematical Physics states, "The entire universe can be regarded as a single quantum system."

Spiritual Sight validates these spiritual understandings and scientific theories. The viewing team directly accesses information from a remote place that can then be verified. This could only be done by the viewing team accessing a universal consciousness that contains all knowledge.

How Does Spiritual Sight Work?

"Human beings have a spiritual dimension that links us with trees and animals, and with each other, with spiritual energies, with discarnate spirits and with God."

--Don Evans, Professor of Philosophy, University of Toronto

In order to understand Spiritual Sight, we must first understand ordinary perception. We do not directly perceive reality. Rather our brains create an approximate image of reality from the billions of bits of information that the mind-brain receives through our five senses. For example, the visual image we call real is created by the brain in a specific area called the occipital lobe. Naturally the actual process is far more complex than the simplistic concept presented here. However the basic concept of vision is that different wavelengths of light strike the back of our eyes and are translated into coded pieces of biological information by the nerve cells of our retinas. This information is then shaped, augmented, and otherwise changed by various substations in the brain. Much of it is discarded before it is finally processed in the occipital lobe.

Our occipital lobe then generates a final image we perceive as being real.

We not only perceive and generate a visual image of reality; we must also learn to interpret it as well. For example, each of us has slight variations in the exact wavelength of light we describe as the color "red". We are trained as children to identify a common visual image as being "red", so that we can interact and communicate with each other within this shared reality. By age five, most of us agree on what is a red color, even though we each may have slight variations of the actual information received from a red object.

The incoming perceptual information, such as a specific wavelength of light, after being encoded as a biological signal, is then mingled with our preconceptions of what we think we should be seeing, our emotions and our memories related to previous encounters with those specific wavelengths of light.

This same general process occurs with all of the five senses, taste, touch, hearing, vision and smell. We also have other important sensory perceptions such as the position of our body in space, and a global sensation of the ambience of a given situation.

All are combined and mingled with memories, emotions and preconceived ideas of what reality should be like, to create the final image we consider to be real. This final mixture we call "shared reality" is about 70% input from our senses and 30% input from memories, emotions and other internal sources.

Spiritual Sight simply takes ordinary sensory perceptions from the remote site and plugs them into this existing neurobiological mind-brain system. Therefore, perceptions from the remote site are also intermingled with memories, emotions and ego-based analysis of what the mind-brain thinks the reality of the remote site should be.

Much of the protocol of Spiritual Sight is to learn how to detach the pure perceptions of the remote site from this inevitable mind-brain overlay of conjecture, memory and other mental associations.

Our ordinary shared reality is naturally very different from a dog's reality or a frog's reality. Each one of us has a different reality from one another. Although the basic components are similar, each person's version of reality can differ from the commonly shared reality, often in significant ways.

We take less than 1% of the billions of bits of information we process through our ordinary senses each second, add a significant amount of preconceived mind-brain information that is unique to a given individual, and then take this distorted fragment of "Everything There Is" to perceive and call it "real".

Of course it is essential that the ego cling tightly to this abbreviated distorted illusion it considers to be real. Children who have had near death experiences tell us that the purpose of life is to learn lessons of love, as this reality is a school. We could not function in our ordinary lives and learn our lessons of love if we were constantly overwhelmed with a shifting massive sensory bombardment of all that there is to perceive.

Buried in this avalanche of ignored sensory information is the energetic signal of perceptions coming from the remote site. The protocol of Spiritual Sight teaches us to let go of our tightly held perception of this local reality and find the series of energetic pulses of information from the remote site. These sensory perceptions from the remote site come to us through our spiritual connection to the creator-God, not from our ordinary senses.

The Spiritual Sight protocol teaches us how to tune in and perceive energetic information from the creative source throughout the course of our ordinary lives. The ego, at times, can be coaxed to be open to beneficial spiritual insights and intuitions which can in turn be helpful to the ego in solving the problems of ordinary living. Meditation is another spiritual practice that can help us to recognize information from the creative source.

When we pray to the creator-God for help and spiritual guidance, we have to be open to the many ways the answers can present themselves to us throughout the course of our daily lives. Spiritual Sight teaches us to hear and appreciate the faint ding of God's angels in our lives.

series of energetic pulses

How Do We Process Information From the Remote Site

"We are not learning to be psychic. We are learning to appreciate ordinary perception."

--Ingo Swann, Psychic and developer of the United States Military's Controlled Remote Viewing program.

We perceive and understand the remote site by using the same mind-brain system we use to perceive our local shared reality. Instead of input from the ordinary sensory systems, the input comes from the Mind of the All, the creator-God.

When we input information, be it from a remote site or our ordinary senses, it has to then be processed and interpreted by the mind-brain. We don't have a separate informational processing system for information from spiritual sources. This is why spiritual visions seem just as real as ordinary perceptions. As one child described his near death experience to me, "It was real, Dr. Morse. It was realer than real."

In order to best explain Spiritual Sight, it must be understood that the mind-brain only has one processing system for perceptual information. Perceptions such as color, taste, sounds and smells can originate from the body's receptors, or from spiritual sources independent of the body.

This is in keeping with many religious traditions, which consider the trinity of the spirit, mind, and the body to represent the totality of man. Please note that what religions call "the mind", this Manual refers to as "the mind-brain".

For example, the New Testament refers to "spirit, mind, and body" as representing the entirety of a given person. (1Thes 5:23[<-]). The Asian tradition of Sukyo Mahikari similarly teaches that man consists of spirit, mind, and body. It is this trinity that connects to the creator-God through the practice of (exchanging light energy) to facilitate that union.

It is also in keeping with the quantum theories in which Consciousness (spirit) observes (mind) and changes properties of reality by just observing it through its (body) receptors.

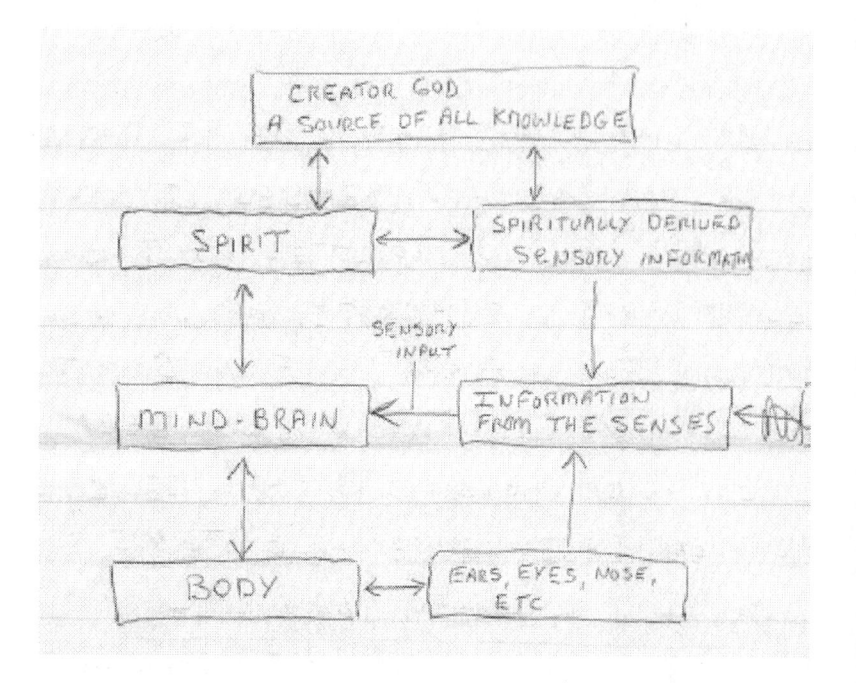

```
           ┌─────────────────────────────┐
           │  CREATOR GOD                │
           │  A SOURCE OF ALL KNOWLEDGE  │
           └─────────────────────────────┘
                ↑↓              ↑↓
  ┌──────────┐         ┌──────────────────────┐
  │  SPIRIT  │ ←─────→ │ SPIRITUALLY DERIVED  │
  │          │         │ SENSORY INFORMATION  │
  └──────────┘         └──────────────────────┘
       ↑↓                SENSORY
                          INPUT
  ┌──────────────┐      ┌──────────────────┐
  │ MIND - BRAIN │ ←─── │ INFORMATION      │ ←── All
  │              │      │ FROM THE SENSES  │
  └──────────────┘      └──────────────────┘
       ↑↓                      ↑
  ┌──────────┐         ┌──────────────────┐
  │  BODY    │ ←─────→ │ EARS, EYES, NOSE,│
  │          │         │ ETC              │
  └──────────┘         └──────────────────┘
```

This model explains the differences between dreams, hallucinations, fantasies, delusions and illusions, from spiritual visions and intuitions.

All are experiences

Spiritual visions and intuitions are the result of normal brain functions and usually well-studied brain structures. See, for example, "Where God Lives" by Melvin Morse and "The Spiritual Brain" by Mario Beauregard.

Dreams and hallucinations arise entirely from the mind-brain without input from the senses, or at best minimal input.

Delusions and illusions do involve a good deal of sensory input but have a greater amount of mind-brain distortion than ordinary perceptions.

Lucid dreams do have the quality of being real, and are speculated to have a strong spiritual component, similar to spiritual visions.

Part of the process of the Spiritual Sight protocol is to learn which perceptions are from the remote site, and which are distortions or inventions of the mind-brain.

"Non-attachment to your own ego lets you fully open the doors of the heart and the windows of perception. When you become *still, zero in your ego, then compassion can flow through you. In that condition, our connection with the universe is changed. It seems like a miracle; but it is actually just a law that connects the formless infinity of creative being with this moment."*

--Yogi Bhajani

The viewer must surrender to the mystery of Spiritual Sight. He or she ideally should simply blurt out whatever thoughts come to mind without internal censorship or process. During stage 2 for example, the monitor will ask, "What are three attributes of the site, three descriptive words, please." The viewer ideally will simply blurt out three words without any further thought process.

The monitor helps the viewer in this process by taking over many of the ego-based executive functions involved in the protocol. The monitor will collect and number the written pages of information about the remote site, as the viewer generates them. The monitor will prompt the viewer to stay on the protocol, organize paperwork, move the viewer around the site and assist with the final summary of information.

This allows the viewer to remain in an ego-less right-brained state of mind and thereby continue to receive clear perceptions from the remote site, relatively unfiltered by the mind-brain.

How Do We Receive Perceptions of a Remote Site?

"Both material reality and spiritual reality have basic structures human beings can discern. One can discern the colors in a rainbow and the spiritual energies in the chakras.

It is true that people of different traditions see colors differently, and that people of different traditions discern spiritual realities differently. The latter occurs, in part, because of the different spiritual language that they use."

--Don Evans

Suppose the remote site is the Eiffel Tower. The Eiffel Tower is a structure made of iron, glass and manmade materials such as concrete, as well as wood and other natural materials.

Each individual material component has its own unique molecular structure emitting a unique energetic signal. Quantum theory dictates that every material has an energetic component at its core.

[Handwritten margin note: We just agree to call it]

The Eiffel Tower has a unique shape. It is a tourist attraction. It has an emotional impact, especially for lovers. It is located in Paris, France, a city known for romance. There have been Hollywood movies, which feature the Eiffel Tower. It is surrounded by souvenir stands. It is in a busy part of Paris, surrounded by cars and city noises. From a distance, at night, its lights can be seen throughout the city and from the air.

All of this is part of what we perceive when we see the Eiffel Tower, either directly or remotely.

The Eiffel Tower has a history that is part of the history of France. The Tower is made of open lattice iron, which presaged a revolution in architectural design.

All this combines to create a complex web of information

associated with the label, "Eiffel Tower." To make the source of this information anonymous for the protocol of Spiritual Sight, we replace the label "Eiffel Tower" with an arbitrary nine-digit number.

All of this interrelated "Eiffel Tower" information is contained in the consciousness of the all-knowing creator God. The arbitrary number or "site address" we have linked to the label "Eiffel Tower" is also contained in in this Universal Consciousness or God.

All of this information can be accessed with the Spiritual Sight protocol by first concentrating on the site address, as we are all spiritually connected to God. In short, we ask God what is the information contained in the Spiritual Sight address, and then receive the basic perceptual information and emotions associated with "Eiffel Tower". We use that information to create an image of the remote site, just as we create our images of directly perceived reality.

Each viewer will react and interact to the "Eiffel Tower"

SPIRITUAL SIGHT – THE MANUAL

packet of information in a different way. An empathetic emotional person might be drawn to the romantic aspects of the Eiffel Tower, and pick up thoughts of honeymooning tourists. An engineer might be drawn to information about the materials and construction of the Tower. Someone interested in history might be drawn to information about its designer, bridge engineer Gustave Eiffel, or the fact that it was the world's tallest building until 1930.

Each viewer accesses unique information from the remote site, and then mingles it with information from their own mind-brain. For example, a romantic person might add information from a favorite Hollywood movie. An engineer, excited by the Eiffel Tower's revolutionary design, might mingle in information about buildings that were influenced by the design of the Eiffel Tower.

The final product is perceived as real by the viewer. The Spiritual Sight protocol is designed to help the viewer-monitor team distinguish which information came from the remote site and what information came from the viewer's mind-brain. There are specific tools and techniques built into the Spiritual Sight protocol to accomplish this all-important goal.

As previously stated, all properly processed sensory information, regardless of its source, be it the spiritual realm or the bodily senses, is then mingled with other mind-brain information.

When we examine an ordinary drinking glass, we feel its hard surface, and see curved lines, transparent and semi-reflective surfaces. We then mingle that sensory information with stored memories of drinking glasses and say, "I have a glass in my hand."

The controlled protocol of Spiritual Sight facilitates taking the viewer's perception of a glass, and breaking it down into the fundamental sensory components that triggered that image.

An example of how spiritual perceptions are combined with mind-brain information comes from the best-selling book,

"The Shack". When the main character finally meets God, he discovers God to have the persona of an African American woman who looks like Oprah. The main character of the book took in spiritual information from the consciousness of the creator-God and mingled it in a unique way with information from his own mind-brain. In doing so, <u>he created a virtual reality he could understand and comfortably interact with.</u>

This is a fictional example of the very real process in which the viewer-monitor team takes spiritually-derived information from the remote site, intermingles it with information from the viewer's mind-brain and creates a virtual reality.

With practice, <u>masters of Spiritual Sight create a virtual reality that is indistinguishable from ordinary reality. They can interact with the remote site in real and verifiable ways.</u> Is this mentally-created virtual reality in fact "real"? There is no definitive answer to that question at this time among masters of Spiritual Sight.

The virtually-created reality of Spiritual Sight mentally

seems to be real. According to Scientific American's Dictionary of Scientific Terminology, reality has its own unique experience that cannot be easily confused with other mental states. Neuroscientists have no standard definition of what reality is. Instead they typically define it as what it is not; that is, for example, reality does not have the same mental characteristics of a dream or drug-induced hallucinations. Reality is generated by normal brain function, as are the virtual realities of Spiritual Sight. Reality has its own unique characteristics, which so far deny a more precise definition.

In addition to having the unique mental sense of being "real," the virtual realities of Spiritual Sight can be validated by actual observation or photographs of the remote site. This is convincing, albeit circumstantial evidence that other spiritual visions and intuitions in general could be real, even if they cannot otherwise be validated.

Granted, as with the virtual reality of Spiritual Sight, spiritual visions can be difficult to interpret because of the comingling of spiritually-derived information with information from the mind-brain. Nevertheless, our ability to validate the spiritually-derived information contained in a Spiritual Sight session strongly suggests that there is in fact a real all-knowing creator-God or universal consciousness.

By "real," the authors of this Manual mean that an all-knowing creator-God exists independent of our individual mind-brains. Our individual mind-brains are part of and continuously interact with the all-knowing creator God as the quantum world's observer and observed are entangled.

Masters of Spiritual Sight can go on to interact with humans, animals and the environment of the remote site. If the remote site is a disease or cancer in a human being, masters of Spiritual Sight can interact with the disease process to better understand it and facilitate healing. True masters of Spiritual Sight work with medical professionals and do not irresponsibly attempt to interact with disease processes without guidance from a patient's personal physician.

The distinction between creating a virtual reality and having an out of body experience becomes blurred for masters of Spiritual Sight. These include Yogis, Brazilian practitioners of spiritism and psychic spies for the United States military intelligence community. Further discussion of the difference between a virtual reality created experience and an out of body experience is outside the scope of this Manual.

As novice practitioners, it is rare to achieve a fully-formed virtual reality at the end of a session. Instead we can expect to receive scattered bits and pieces of information from the remote site.

Think of the protocol as using the viewer's mind-brain to access a faint radio signal from God or a universal consciousness. Masters of Spiritual Sight call this faint signal the "signal line." Ultimately the goal of Spiritual Sight is to learn to identify God's signal line for us in our ordinary lives.

The signal line is the totality of information streaming from the remote site. As previously discussed, the information from the Eiffel Tower would include its iron structure, distinctive shape, location in Paris, the thoughts of visitors, the thoughts of Parisians who view it at night, the vendors and customers of the souvenir stands surrounding it, honking horns, traffic sounds, the anxieties, fears and enjoyment of people at the top, the claustrophobia of being in the elevator, among many other bits of information streaming from the site.

Our brains routinely process billions of bits of information, so the information contained in the Spiritual Sight digital address for "Eiffel Tower" is easily lost in all the information the mind-brain routinely processes. The mind-brain has over a billion neuronal connections as well as proteins and hormones, which convey information.

The information streaming in from the remote site has to compete for the mind-brain's attention with the billions of bits of information streaming in each second from the ordinary senses. The signal line from a remote site is faint. There is an overwhelming amount of background noise. This is what is meant by the "faint ding" of God's voice in our lives.

As previously stated, our mind-brain only uses a small amount of this deluge of information to create its perception of ordinary reality.

Throughout the process of Spiritual Sight, we must sift through billions of bits of information competing for the mind-brain's attention in order find the signal line of the remote site. Information from the signal line will often seem odd, bizarre, and unexpected, as it is not the ordinary perceptual information the mind-brain analyzes. In general, intuitive information often seems odd, uncomfortable or unreal.

A good analogy is our efforts to tune a radio to a far away radio signal. Initially we might just get interrupted bursts of faint information. We might get a feeble, blurred, static-filled transmission. Occasionally the signal will be very loud and clear. Often we will get garbled sentences without supporting context. With practice, we get better and better at both tuning the radio and interpreting the transmissions.

Novices of Spiritual Sight frequently start off with fuzzy and blurred images of the remote site. Often fully-formed images are created by the mind-brain in its efforts to understand the remote site. They can be very clear and seem real, yet be completely inaccurate. The Spiritual Sight protocol specifically deals with this challenge and resolves it.

Ultimately, masters of Spiritual Sight create a virtual image that cannot easily be distinguished from the actual site. They can visit and interact with the site.

What is the Role of the Monitor?

"If you believe yourself worthy of the thing you fought so hard to get, then you become an instrument of God, you help the soul of the world and you understand why you are here."

--Paulo Coelho, Warrior of Light

1. <u>Tuning the viewer:</u> The monitor observes and "tunes" the viewer as one might tune a radio receiver. The tasks of Spiritual Sight are to both access the signal line of the remote site and to learn to interpret it. The viewer gives off subtle

tells such as a certain tone of voice, hand movements, facial expressions and other unconscious cues during the viewing. With experience, the monitor can learn to interpret these cues. Sometimes they will correlate with highly accurate information from the remote site. Other times they will be associated with recognizable distortions of the signal line. They can also indicate that the viewer has missed the remote site completely. If this happens, and the monitor recognizes a characteristic tell by the viewer meaning the viewer is off signal, the monitor can redirect the viewer by having him or her retake the site address.

For example, a common tell that highly accurate information has come through from the remote site is a note of surprise in the viewer's voice. A common tell associated with totally missing the signal line is for the viewer to unconsciously shake his or her head "no", while describing the remote site.

2. Prompting the viewer: The monitor typically prompts the viewer through the various stages of the protocol. It is important that the viewer say all thoughts out loud so that the monitor knows where the viewer is with regards to the various steps and stages of the protocol.

For example, the monitor might say, "Now I will give you the site address," or "Is the remote site a place – water or land, something man made, biological or aerial?"

The monitor might say, "What colors do you see?", "What smells do you smell", or "Are you indoors or outdoors?" The viewer speaks all thoughts out loud so that the monitor doesn't ask about colors when the viewer is experiencing smells and disrupt the orderly flow of information.

The monitor must be careful to ask open-ended questions such as, "What sounds do you hear?" or broad fixed-choice question such as "Is it hot, warm, cool or cold?" to avoid contaminating the session.

Another properly phrased question is "Reach down and tell me what, if anything, you feel." Always give the viewer the option to not have any experience so that the viewer's mind-brain does not invent something to fulfill a perceived expectation.

3. Moving around the site: The monitor can move the viewer around the site to explore it. For example, "Move 500 feet in the air, look down, and sketch what you see," or "Move five feet in front of the person at the site and tell me what colors you see." Detailed and precise instructions yield the most

accurate information. For example, it is typically preferable to ask, "What sounds do you hear?" than to say, "Describe the remote site."

4. <u>The monitor can be the viewer's left brain:</u> The more left brain tasks the monitor can do for the viewer, the better. The viewer can number the pages of data, organize the incoming information, and help the viewer adhere to the protocol. The more left-brained tasks the monitor performs, the more likely it is that the viewer will remain in a right-brained receptive frame of mind. The monitor can also suggest when to take a break. Typically <u>the most accurate information comes to the viewer after a short break.</u>

Sometimes the viewer will completely enter into a trance state, and be unable to write or speak. The monitor can gently bring the viewer partially out of this state so that the flow of information from the site continues to be documented. The monitor, in this situation, might actually write the information while the viewer says it out loud. This is unusual. It is preferable that the viewer both speak all thoughts out loud and write them down in the protocol format, which will be described later in the Manual.

Common Pitfalls of the Process

"Before embarking on an important battle, a warrior of light asks himself: "How far have I developed my abilities?" He knows he has learned something with every battle he has fought. Victors never make the same mistake twice. That is why the warrior only risks his heart for something worthwhile."

--Paulo Coelho, The Warrior of Light

1. <u>The viewer must be alert and communicate all thoughts to the monitor:</u> It cannot be repeated enough that the viewer say all thoughts out loud, throughout the process. All thoughts, no matter how fleeting, meaningless, absurd, or seemingly

irrelevant must be verbalized. The viewer must strive to not analyze, filter, or censor the flow of information. He or she ideally should relax and surrender to the process. Often the most overlooked pieces of information, will, during the feedback session, turn out to be the most meaningful. All viewers have had the experience of, upon learning the nature of the remote site, suddenly remember something pertinent they did not express during the session. Such details remembered after the session is complete do not contribute to the learning process, which is the purpose of the protocol.

2. The viewer should strive to not interpret the information or name the remote site: It is only natural that the viewer will both access this signal line and attempt to interpret the incoming

information. Such efforts can distort the flow of information. The viewer might then invent sensory impressions to fit this preconceived idea of the nature of the remote site. The viewer's ego wants to be correct in its assessment of the remote site and will invent information.

This same process occurs commonly in ordinary life. Often we are faced with new situations. Our egos, in an effort to control the situation, will invent perception, often based on fears and anxieties. Learning to identify this process when it occurs during a Spiritual Sight session will help us navigate ego-driven anxieties and fears in everyday life.

Fear is often properly known as "False Evidence Appearing Real."

The point of Spiritual Sight is not to become skilled at identifying the remote site, but to become skilled at identifying our ego's well-meaning distortions and falsifications of our ordinary thought processes.

When distortions and inventions of the signal line occur in the Spiritual Sight process, the monitor can gently redirect the ego. For example, the monitor can say, "Good job Ego, thank you. <u>That was a valid insight of what might be going on. Now let's try to identify the sensory information that led you to such a conclusion.</u>" This same approach can be used for ego-driven fears and anxieties that occur in ordinary thoughts throughout our daily lives.

3. <u>The viewer can correctly identify the remote site:</u>
Another common pitfall occurs when the viewer correctly identifies the remote site. The ego is now firmly back in control of the process. This can shorten the viewing. As a result, the flow of information might cease. The viewer may not be

able to construct a detailed enough virtual reality to progress to interacting with the site.

The purpose of Spiritual Sight is to learn to have a dialog with the creator-God. Quickly identifying the remote site can result in abruptly ending the communication with the Mind of the All or Universal Consciousness.

4. Not understanding the role of the monitor: Of course many people remote view or do Spiritual Sight entirely by themselves, functioning as both monitor and viewer. However, masters of Spiritual Sight, who include Brazilian and Yogi practitioners, believe that viewer-monitor teams generally outperform single viewers working alone. This is also supported by the experience of the highly successful psychic spy programs in both the United States and Russia.

The monitor can help the viewer adhere to the protocol, recognize the viewer's tells and help avoid common pitfalls. The dialog between the viewer and monitor enriches the spiritual dimension of what otherwise can be a narrow demonstration of psychic talent.

Applications for Spiritual Healing

"Now a centurion had a servant who was sick and at the point of death, who was highly valued by him. When the centurion heard about Jesus, he sent to him elders of the Jews, asking him to come and heal his servant... And Jesus went with them. When he was not far from the house, the centurion sent friends, saying to him, "Lord do not trouble yourself, for I am not worthy to have you come under my roof. But say the word and let my servant be healed... And when those who had been sent returned to the house, they found the servant well."

--Luke 7:2-10

Perhaps the most sacred and yet practical application for

Spiritual Sight is its use in spiritual and energetic healing. This program has been specifically designed for a complementary role with medical professionals.

The quote from the New Testament written over 2,000 years ago is one of the oldest documented cases of spiritual healing at a distance. More recently, Elizabeth Fischer Targ published an article in the Western Journal of Medicine documenting the positive effects of distance healing on AIDS patients. Spiritual Sight has its roots in the healing practices of the Japanese Art of Reiki, as developed by Usui-Sensei in the early 1900's in Japan.

Only masters of Spiritual Sight are qualified to be engaged in spiritual healing. They uniformly work closely with physicians and other health practitioners. Spirituality is an essential component to all aspects of medical practice. The authors of this Manual specifically reject the "either-or" unhealthy divisive mentality that is sometimes seen between those interested in spiritual aspects of medical practice and those interested and adept at the biomechanical arts of medical practice.

We teach from the start the rigorous best practices of Spiritual Sight anticipating that some will progress to spiritual healing as an adjunct therapy in medical practice.

Treating patients as a "whole" is fundamental in many medical specialties such as Homeopathy. Very well developed in Europe, Homeopathy has a "Body-Mind-spirit" approach that gathers total information data from a patient, which in return allows the physician to tackle the root causes of ailments and illnesses. It is not only applicable to human medicine but also to animals as doctors in veterinary medicine in Europe use the holistic approach on pet patients and obtain tremendous results.

The Spiritual Sight Protocol

"In general, life energies and spirits seem just as real to me as desks and sounds. In a genuine spiritual experience, there are often elements that can be confirmed by ordinary sense experience."

--Don Evans

Initially, new practitioners of Spiritual Sight learn a strict yet simple protocol. This makes it easier for novices to gain rudimentary skills at Spiritual Sight, for the straight-forward reason that the protocol works. Almost anyone who carefully follows the Spiritual Site protocol will have gratifying results. The protocol can be learned within several hours. New practitioners can be confident that they will have verifiable interactions with the creator-God if they can surrender to the demands of the protocol. These demands are the basics of man-God interactions, specifically, mental discipline, surrendering the ego, surrendering to the mystery of the Universe, meditation, and a willingness to be wrong.

Learning the basic protocol makes it easier to work with different partners in viewer-monitor teams. The two people need to trust each other and have open clear communications. Even slight variations in style and/or language use can be very disruptive to the functioning of the viewer-monitor team.

After novices become more experienced, and viewer-monitor teams learn the basics of Spiritual Sight, they typically will modify the protocol to suit their individual practices. Some viewers, for example, prefer to dictate the sensory information to the monitor, instead of writing it down themselves. Other viewer-monitor teams create their own systems to sort and organize the incoming sensory information to best fit their own mental styles of practice.

It is important to first master the protocol as it was developed. It represents over twenty years of tedious trial and error testing. The Spiritual Sight protocol is based on the highly successful protocols of Brazilian spiritists and U.S. military psychic spies. Each represents decades of experience in the spiritual art of remote viewing.

Masters of Spiritual Sight alter the protocol to fit their individual strengths and weaknesses as both viewers and monitors. Teams receive immediate feedback at the end of a session, so they can assess for themselves what worked and what did not contribute to a successful viewing. Success, for a Spiritual Sight session is defined as an interaction with the creator-God that produced unequivocal independently-verified evidence of that encounter.

Spiritual Sight sessions are termed "direct hits," "site contact" or "misses". A direct hit is when a third party observer can read the target summary, review the site photographs and acknowledge the summary clearly and distinctly describes the remote site. Site contact is when the target summary describes the remote site, but in a general or vague way. It can clearly be distinguished from most possible sites, but could apply to several similar sites. A miss is when the summary could apply to a multitude of remote sites or has elements not found or contradicted by the specific features of the remote site.

Ordinary common sense can be used to assess the outcome of a Spiritual Sight session. If there are any doubts, simply ask a non-involved third party to review the session and photographs of the remote site. It is rare for there to be significant controversy over the result of a session. If there is doubt as to the outcome, simply ignore the session for feedback purposes and do another one.

The protocol was specifically adapted for spiritual and healing purposes from the open source controlled remote viewing protocol developed at the Stanford Research Institute by psychic Ingo Swann and theoretical physicist Hal Puthoff. It was developed for use by the United States government and was declassified after 20 years of rigorous scientific testing. Virtually all of the military psychic spies became profoundly spiritually transformed by their practice of controlled remote viewing. The CRV protocol was designed for persons with no known or apparent psychic abilities.

As with any skill, such as hitting a baseball or drawing a picture, it is important to first learn the basics. Of course there will always be highly gifted individuals who transcend the need for learning basic skills. Individual variations in technique naturally occur as practitioners become more proficient. However even masters of Spiritual Sight return to the fundamentals of the protocol if they are experiencing difficulties with their sessions, to regain their mastery of the process.

Mental Discipline is Required

"... the mind is restless, turbulent, strong and unyielding ... as difficult to subject as the wind."

-- Bhagavad Gita

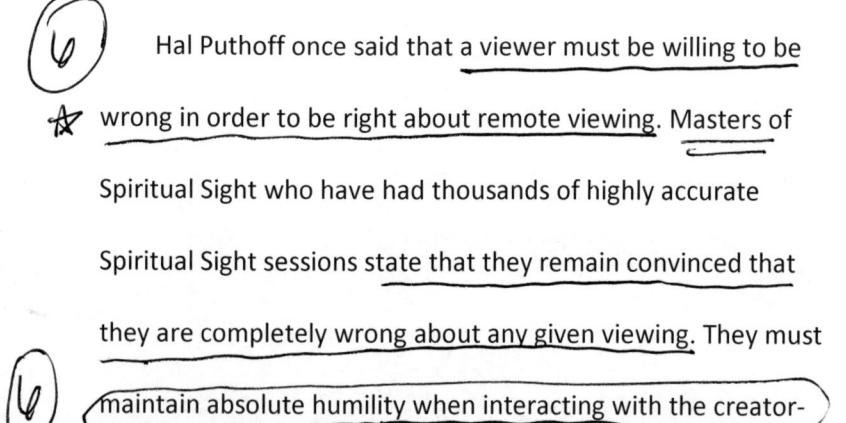

Hal Puthoff once said that a viewer must be willing to be wrong in order to be right about remote viewing. Masters of Spiritual Sight who have had thousands of highly accurate Spiritual Sight sessions state that they remain convinced that they are completely wrong about any given viewing. They must maintain absolute humility when interacting with the creator-God. It is hard to imagine how someone can maintain total humility after numerous highly successful sessions, yet it must be done. As soon as a practitioner becomes certain they have correctly identified a remote site, they almost certainly have missed the site completely.

The ego interferes with successful viewings. The ego clings tightly to its grip on this local reality we all share. It wants to be in control and always right in its perception of reality. That is the ego's job, so it is natural that it also wants to control and be accurate in its assessment of the remote site. We all want to hear God's voice in our lives, yet we also often want to control what God has to say to us and what God's plan is for our individual lives.

It is the ego's job to create our perceptions of reality so that we can properly function in our everyday lives. It is hard work and requires mental discipline to get the ego to stand down even for the brief period of time involved in a Spiritual Sight session.

It is the ego's role to filter and shape the billions of bits of information that we are bombarded with every second and create a stable reality for us to function in. We must honor the ego and acknowledge its difficult role in providing a stable reality. We cannot learn our lessons of love or function as capable human beings without strong capable egos.

Tibetan monk Pema Chadron teaches that we must be willing to experience loss, and to suffer, in order for the ego to loosen its grip on reality. It is those times when the ego temporarily becomes overwhelmed, confused, or even obliterated, that we experience opportunities for spiritual advancement.

Spiritual Sight is an opportunity for the ego to stand down in a controlled situation, to peel back our illusionary self-created reality, to experience genuine communication with the creative source of all that is real. We can then return rejuvenated and inspired to better participate in this illusionary realm we consider to be real.

One essential mental discipline is for the viewer to suspend judgment and analysis for the short period of time of a Spiritual

Sight session. It requires considerable mental discipline to simply allow the flood of information stream into our minds directly from the creator-God. This fundamental spiritual skill can be learned by practicing Spiritual Sight.

One must learn to trust God in order to successfully advance as a master of Spiritual Sight who otherwise has no expectation of success. One must learn to ask the ego to stand down, avoid judgment and analysis, and yet faithfully report to the monitor all thoughts out loud. It is as simple and as easy and as ultimately difficult as that.

Surrender to the mystery of the protocol. One master of Spiritual Sight told me that her abilities came from the complete freedom from responsibility that came from recognizing that she did not have to be good at Spiritual Sight, she had only to experience the process. "For the first time in my life I could just be, and not worry if I was right or wrong. Spiritual Sight allows me to be free from constantly judging myself."

Spiritual Sight: A Spiritual Tuning Fork

The smallest inner voice

Is that of the master.

This is the voice of the universe.

When you identify with this voice

Your will becomes congruent

With the will of the universe.

This is the voice incapable of giving

You bad advice.

--Bill Harvey, Mind Magic

SPIRITUAL SIGHT – THE MANUAL

During Spiritual Sight, we access verifiable information from the consciousness of the creative universe. This is also the source of intuition and spiritual inspiration in general.

We can then compare what it is like to obtain information from the creator-God with the perceptions of information collected by our ordinary senses. In this manner we can learn how to best access, identify, and process other messages from the creator-God.

Each one of us has a different reaction to information and messages from God. For some, there is a distinct yet indescribable sense of certainty to contact with the divine. This is that odd sense of confidence masters of Spiritual Sight have when they are never certain or feel "right" yet have confidence in being wrong. Novices will experience this as they become more proficient at Spiritual Sight. For others, there is a distinct uncertainty to the experience of genuine communication with God. For most, the experience is odd, unfamiliar, at times humorous and even absurd.

Module "Embracing Uncertainty"

"Angels are real, powerful, and often very funny."

--Pierre Jovanovic, Investigations into Angel Encounters

Learning how the information from Spiritual Sight presents itself to you can help to identify the guidance of God in our everyday lives. Masters of Spiritual Sight call this "finding the signal line of our own personal spiritual journey."

The Stages of Spiritual Sight

"Enlightenment is consciousness of a state of direct knowledge of yourself as you truly are."

--Unknown spiritual master

The experience of direct knowledge is just "knowing," the way that you know anything that requires no thought process. For example, your name, where the kitchen is in your house, or the names of household furniture. When we think of how we know something, we usually think of receiving information through our senses and processing it with our brains. "Knowing" often is a past memory of something we have previously experienced.

There is also a realm of intuitive knowledge, where the intrinsic fundamental ability of each of us to directly "know" is timeless. It is not dependent on specific past memories. It is exercised in the eternal realm of the true individual.

Spiritual Sight can lead directly to enlightenment as part of this process of entering into the realm of intuitive knowledge.

Intuition is the power of the mind by which it immediately knows the truth of reality without reasoning or analysis.

"The warrior of light knows the importance of intuition. The warrior of light knows that intuition is God's language and he continues listening to the wind and talking to the stars."

--Paulo Coelho

Neale Donald Walsch, in "Conversations with God" quotes God as saying to him:

"Ask me anything. Anything. I will contrive to bring you the answer. The whole universe I will use to do this. So be on the lookout. Watch. Listen. The words in the next song you hear. The information in the next article you read. The story line of the next movie you watch. The chance utterance of the next person you meet. Or the whisper of the next river, the next ocean, the next breeze that caresses your ear – all these devices are mine; all these avenues are open to me. I will speak to you if you listen."

Ultimately spiritual Sight is about learning to listen to the universe as it speaks to us in our ordinary lives. We learn to distinguish the chaos of the universe from authentic communications born of the hidden order of the creator-God. The former are born of fear and anxiety. True communications to us born of intuition come from the suspension of ego, judgment and analysis.

The protocol of Spiritual Sight teaches us to distinguish fear- and anxiety-based thoughts from those free of judgment, ego and analysis.

The Remote Site Address: Spiritual Sight Involves Asking God a Very Specific Question

The Spiritual Sight protocol asks God a very specific question: "What is the exact nature of a person, place, or thing that cannot be accessed by ordinary perception or memory?"

The remote site (the person, place, or thing) is given a nine-digit number so it has an identifying address. The number is the site address for the entire energetic signal and bundled information that is the remote site. The identifying number is arbitrary, selected at random by the facilitator of the Spiritual Sight protocol for a given viewer-monitor team.

For example, suppose the facilitator has chosen the Eiffel Tower for the team to view. The number 698437869 might be selected to represent the energy signature of the Eiffel Tower.

The team is given this number and no other information about the remote site, at the beginning of a session.

Depending on the experience of the team and the specific

goals of a training session, the monitor may or may not know the identity of the remote site. Typically, a third party, otherwise not involved in the session, will select the remote site and give the nine-digit address to the team. However there are circumstances where the monitor will select the target and the site address for a session. When this occurs, the monitor must be careful as to not influence the viewer throughout the session. Often when the monitor is aware of the identity of the remote site unconscious cues from the monitor can contaminate the viewing process. The protocol is specifically designed to minimize the chances of this happening.

Both types of sessions have their own unique value.

When both monitor and viewer are learning the basics of Spiritual Sight, it is often helpful if a third party chooses the remote site for them. The team only knows the numeric site address. It is generally helpful to inform the team of a vague general category of information that the site belongs to. This will be discussed in greater detail in the section on Stage 2.

Melvin L. Morse, M.D. and Isabelle Chauffeton Saavedra

When the monitor is already a master of Spiritual Sight, or very experienced with the protocol, often it is beneficial for the monitor to know the details of the remote site. These sessions are helpful to 1) Train the viewer, but not the monitor, in the process, or 2) Train the team to work together as a smoothly functioning unit.

For example, suppose a specific viewer is excellent at remote sites involving buildings, but challenged at viewing people. The monitor can choose remote sites involving people to give the viewer more experience in that facet of the process.

It must always be remembered that the goal of Spiritual Sight is to learn to listen for the voice of the creator-God, not to identify by name a remote site. Ideally the viewer-monitor team will generate a detailed description, with sketches, of the remote site and yet otherwise not be able to identify it by name or location.

— like me working w/ Gary's A-Team

Brief Overview of the Four Stages of Spiritual Sight

Hey, Er...." Said Zaphod. "What's your name?" The man looked at him doubtfully. "I don't know. Why, do you think I should have one? It seems very odd to give a bundle of vague sensory perceptions a name."

--Doug Adams (The Restaurant at the End of the Universe)

Stage 1: Preparing the mind

Stage 2: Initial contact with the informational energy signal of the site

Stage 3: Accessing sensory information from the site. Sifting true information from the site from ego-based, emotional, and random stray informational noise coming from the mind-brain.

Experiencing the emotional impact of the site

Stage 4: Sketching the site

Stage 3 continues throughout stage 4.

Creating a summary of the remote site.

End of session.

All information gathered during the process is important. For Spiritual Sight this means all mental processes experienced by the viewer are essential pieces of the process. The viewer ideally should speak out loud and jot down all thoughts, no matter how unrelated or inconsequential they may appear. The monitor helps the viewer, by prompting the various stages of the protocol, and recording and organizing all information.

The viewer can relax into the process and feel confident that if he or she simply shares all thoughts with the monitor, the remote site will be described and communication with the creator-God achieved.

Spiritual Sight involves accessing information directly from the creator consciousness. Speculations by the viewer and/or monitor risk limiting or contaminating the process. Patience is an essential skill for successful Spiritual Sight.

In the Jewish religion it is forbidden to even have a name for the creator-God. Attempting to name God ultimately limits our understanding of God. Devout Jews often write the name of the Divine as G-d. This is why, throughout this Manual, we use a variety of different names to identify the ultimately unknowable source of life, consciousness and creation.

Of course after a session is complete, most viewer-monitor teams are eager to learn the identity of the remote site. Immediate feedback, either by visiting the remote site or reviewing photographs, is typically given at the end of a session.

The flexible protocol of Spiritual Sight teaches mental discipline yet allows for individual spiritual styles in both viewer and monitor. Without the protocol, mental discipline, as well as the ability of the individuals to work together as a spiritual team, is easily lost.

When we limit our understanding of the creator-God's message for us, we limit our own spiritual development.

It takes patience and mental discipline to both surrender to the protocol of Spiritual Sight and to surrender to God's plan for our spiritual journey in this human existence.

As in our previous example of viewing the Eiffel Tower, the viewer-monitor team could easily feel gratification and pride at concluding it is the Seattle Space Needle, as the session unfolds. After all the Space Needle is very similar to the Eiffel Tower.

The team will miss out on the romance, charm and unique history of the Eiffel Tower. They will not have the experience of speaking non-verbally to French-speaking Parisians. Much is lost by prematurely attempting to identify the site.

When we limit our understanding of the creator-God, we

limit our own spiritual development.

"Ego less ness is a state of mind that has complete confidence in the sacredness of the world."

--Pema Chodrom

Specific Descriptions of Each of the Stages of Spiritual Sight

"The way involves respect for all small and subtle things. Learn to recognize the right moment to adopt the necessary attitudes."

--Lao Tzu

Spiritual Sight is a controlled process consisting of <u>flexible yet rigorous stages.</u>

Stage 1: Preparing the Mind

"Every second of the search is an encounter with God."

Paulo Coelho

See diagram 1, Stage 1, Step 1:

```
                                    NAME
                                    DATE
                                    TIME
                                    PLACE
                                    MONITOR'S
                                       NAME
                                    2-5 Word
                                    Description of
                                    Surroundings
```

DIAGRAM 1   STAGE 1   Step 1

SPIRITUAL SIGHT – THE MANUAL

Step 1: A brief left-brain exercise to honor the ego. Successful Spiritual Sight involves asking the ego to relax its tight grip on reality, to let the faint voice of the creator-God intrude into our firmly-fixed image of reality.

This first step is to honor the left brain and engage it in the process.

At the top right hand corner of the page, the viewer writes and says out loud his or her name, the date, the time, the place, the name of the monitor, and a brief description of the surroundings.

For example, if the authors of this Manual were starting a session, the viewer might list, Melvin Morse; July 6, 2014; 3:30 pm; Orlando, Florida, USA; Isabelle is monitor; Isabelle's living room.

Many spiritual traditions begin prayer sessions with a similar recitation of left brain exercises to first firmly ground the practitioner in the ordinary reality around us.

For example Japanese practitioners of Sukyo Mahikari begin their monthly meetings with a recitation of the time and place of the meeting and the relationship of the local organization to the national and then international organizations.

[Margin note: Yes! Wow!]

Just as we might tense a muscle as a prelude to relaxing it, we ask the ego to flex its mental muscles before then asking it to relax its grip on our mind-brain functions.

Step 2: Meditation

[Margin note: Do this! 5-20 minutes]

The viewer now meditates for five minutes at a minimum, preferably 20 minutes. The viewer should use whatever meditative techniques work for the viewer. Some viewers simply let their minds go blank. Others do active meditative practices. Listening to music is common practice, but there is no one meditative technique that works better than another.

Research documents that some sort of mediation is very

beneficial to the process.

In fact, meditation is the single most effective way to tame the left mind-brain and to keep it under control. Meditation that incorporates rhythmic or Pranayama breathing is particularly effective as the sound of breathing gives the left brain something to focus on, something to nibble on, freeing the right brain from the constant surveillance from its neighbor. Once the left brain is distracted and loses its grip and control, right brain can "escape" and connect with the creative source.

If the viewer is unfamiliar to mediation, here are two useful methods.

1) <u>Focusing on the breath:</u> Sit comfortably on a chair or cross-legged on the floor. Use pillows if helpful. Fold your hands in your lap. Focus on your breathing.

Breathe at a normal pace. Breathe through the nose with the mouth closed. Actively think "breathing out" and "breathing in" or "out" and "in". When thoughts come to mind, do not judge them or judge yourself for having them. Simply think, "Thinking, oh, I am thinking". Then return to the breath.

The monitor can keep track of the time and prompt the next step. Viewer and monitor can decide in advance how long the mediation should last. Or, the viewer can decide to end the meditation step and move on.

2. Chanting a mantra: One commonly used mantra comes from the Kundalini Yogic tradition. Again, the viewer sits comfortably. He or she chants, "Sat nam".

"Sat nam" means "truth is his name". It is a sound embodiment of the word of God that lives inside each of us. Yogi Bahjan, who popularized Kundalini Yoga for the West, says this of the sat nam mantra: "Sat nam tunes into the divine infinity. It will take the mind and heart to an experience of its origin in the creator."

Breathe slowly in through the nose. Then exhale while chanting "Sa-a-a-at nam". The ratio of sat to nam is 8 counts to

1. Don't worry about precisely chanting it correctly. Find a rhythm that feels right to you. Simply chant a long drawn out "Sa-a-a-at" followed by a short "nam".

Then briefly pause and inhale.

As with the first technique, the monitor and viewer together decide on the length of meditation.

In some cases, when the viewer becomes more proficient in Spiritual Sight, he or she can choose to meditate alone, before even starting a session or a viewing. In that case, STAGE 1 will go directly from Step 1 to Step 3 and 4 and so on to the other stages, marking just a short pause with a couple of deep breaths to reaffirm the state of mind between Step 1 and Step 3 of STAGE ONE. At any given time during the viewing, the viewer can decide to go back to meditation if he or she feels the need to re-anchor his or her connectedness to the Universe.

Step 3: Opening the Channel

The viewer identifies, says out loud, and documents any mental barriers to a viewing. The monitor prompts the viewer by asking, "Do you have any mental roadblocks to a successful viewing?" The viewer will then both say any mental roadblocks out loud and briefly jot them down in the top left hand corner of the Stage 1 paper. (See diagram 2, Stage 1, Step 3)

SPIRITUAL SIGHT – THE MANUAL

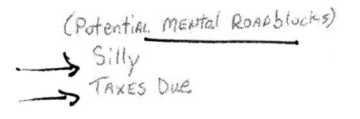

(Potential MENTAL ROADblocks)
→ Silly
→ TAXES Due

Melvin Morse
July 6 2013
3:30 pm
Orlando
FLORIDA, USA
Monitor: Isabelle
Isabelle's Living Room

DIAGRAM 2 Stage 1 Step 3

Diagram 2, Stage 1, Step 3

Melvin L. Morse, M.D. and Isabelle Chauffeton Saavedra

DISTRACTIONS

If there are no mental roadblocks, the viewer replies "none" and does not write anything down. If there are no mental roadblocks, the top left hand corner of the page is left blank.

If there are mental roadblocks, they should be briefly noted in one to three words.

For example:

Monitor: "Do you have any mental roadblocks to a successful viewing?"

Viewer: "Yes I think this is silly."

The viewer then writes "silly" in the top left hand corner.

"Also I am worried about paying my taxes."

The viewer lists "taxes" under "silly".

"Also I keep thinking about my son who was arrested for possession of marijuana last week."

The viewer then lists "son's arrest" under the other entries.

The monitor and the viewer then set aside each roadblock. This is a formal process addressing each roadblock using the phrase "set aside".

Just before surrender

For example the monitor might say:

1) This protocol does seem silly, but we know it works so we will set that concern aside.

2) This problem with taxes is of course worrisome but cannot be resolved in the next hour, so we will set it aside.

3) It certainly is troubling that your son was arrested, but we will set it aside for the next hour and have a successful viewing.

Each potential roadblock is acknowledged, honored, and ultimately set aside.

Masters of Spiritual Sight typically list and set aside five to ten potential roadblocks.

As one master of Spiritual Sight is fond of saying,

"Unexpressed mental roadblocks corrupt the signal line."

Step 4: Premonitions of the Remote Site

The monitor now asks, "Do you (the viewer) have any premonitions of the remote site?"

The viewer will often have visual images and/or ideas about the remote site. They are expressed and documented at this time. Often viewers have left over imagery from a previous session, especially if it was successful at describing the remote site. (All sessions are learning experiences and by definition are all successful in that regard.)

It does not matter if the advance premonitions are correct or not. Some are; most are not.

Spiritual Sight is a controlled process with an orderly flow of information. Correctly identifying the identity of the remote site too soon in the process can stunt the spiritual experience.

Premonitions of the remote site are verbally expressed and recorded at this step. They are then set aside. No judgment or analysis should be attached to them.

If there are advanced premonitions, the viewer states them out loud and jots one or two words in the space just below the mental roadblocks. (See diagram 3, Stage 1, Step 4)

For example if the remote site is the Eiffel Tower, common premonitions might include "tall structure" or "big city." "Sail boat" or "water" might just as easily be present.

If there are no advanced premonitions of the remote site, the space is left blank.

Silly
Taxes due

(Examples of premonitions)
Tall structure
Big city
Sail Boat
WATER

Melvin Morse
July 6 2013
3:30 pm
Orlando
Florida, USA
Monitor: Isabelle
Isabelle's living Room

DIAGRAM 3 Stage 1 Step 4

Diagram 3, Stage 1, Step 4

Stage 2: First Contact

"The way involves respect for all small and subtle things. Learn to recognize the right moment to adopt the necessary attitudes."

--Lao Tzu

Ideally this entire stage should be brief, without much time for thought. Masters of Spiritual Sight often complete the entire stage in one to three minutes.

Again, all thoughts are said out loud. If the stage takes too long (five or ten minutes) or there is too much off-signal thinking, the monitor might decide to repeat the stage.

The art of being a monitor is, in part, to decide when the viewer might be slightly off protocol, but still on the signal line, versus when the viewer needs to retake the site address and reset.

The monitor can make the best decisions for the team if there is trust between monitor and viewer and the viewer says all thoughts out loud.

With practice, stage 2 will flow smoothly and quickly, without extra thought.

Masters of Spiritual Sight, when having difficulties with their practice, will return to stage 2 and practice it again and again until it feels smooth and continuous.

Step 1: The Site Address

The site address is a nine-digit number that links the information of the remote site to the viewer's mind. It is the address of the site in the Mind of the All.

The monitor recites the address. The viewer writes it down and says the numbers out loud.

The target number can be recited as three blocks of three numbers. Nine digits was chosen so that the viewer knows how

SPIRITUAL SIGHT – THE MANUAL

many numbers to expect and can anticipate the end of the

sequence of numbers. (See diagram 4, Stage 2, Step 1)

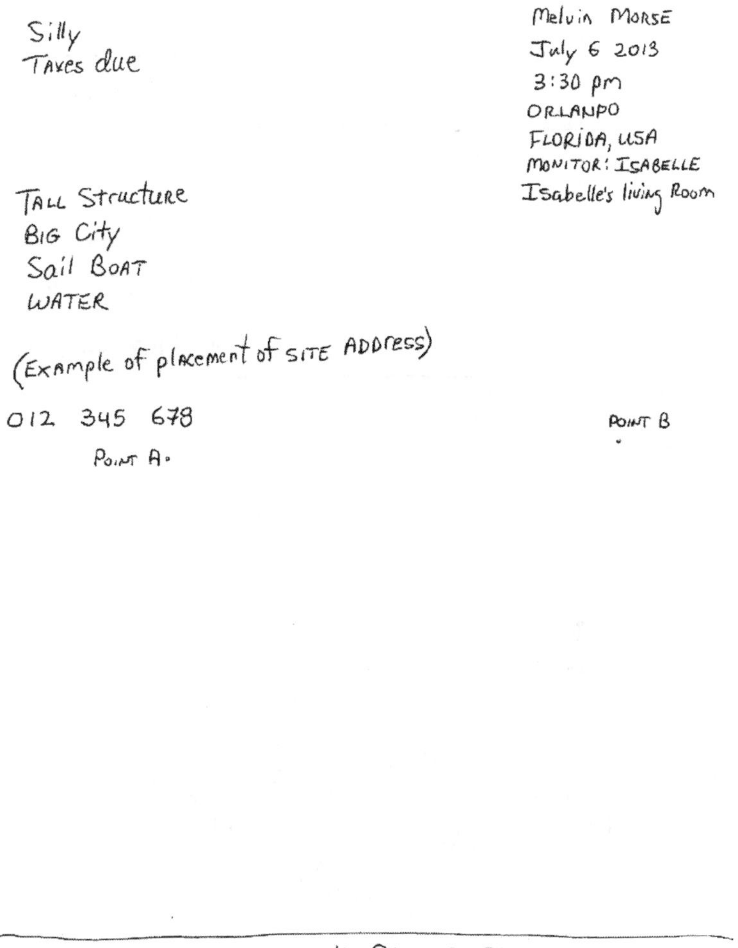

Silly
Taxes due

Melvin Morse
July 6 2013
3:30 pm
Orlando
Florida, USA
Monitor: Isabelle
Isabelle's living Room

Tall Structure
Big City
Sail Boat
Water

(Example of placement of site Address)

012 345 678
   Point A.

Point B

Diagram 4 Stage 2 Step 1

Diagram 4, Stage 3, Step 1

Step 2: First Energetic Contact (Diagram 5)

Step 2 is often compared to putting one's finger in a light socket and getting a mild electric shock. It represents the first energetic contact with the remote site.

Immediately after the viewer writes the last digit of the site address, he or she puts the pen on Point A (See diagram 5). The hand then moves of its own accord, without thought by the viewer, creating a line, ending at point B.

A → B helpful for mediumship?
"energetic contact"

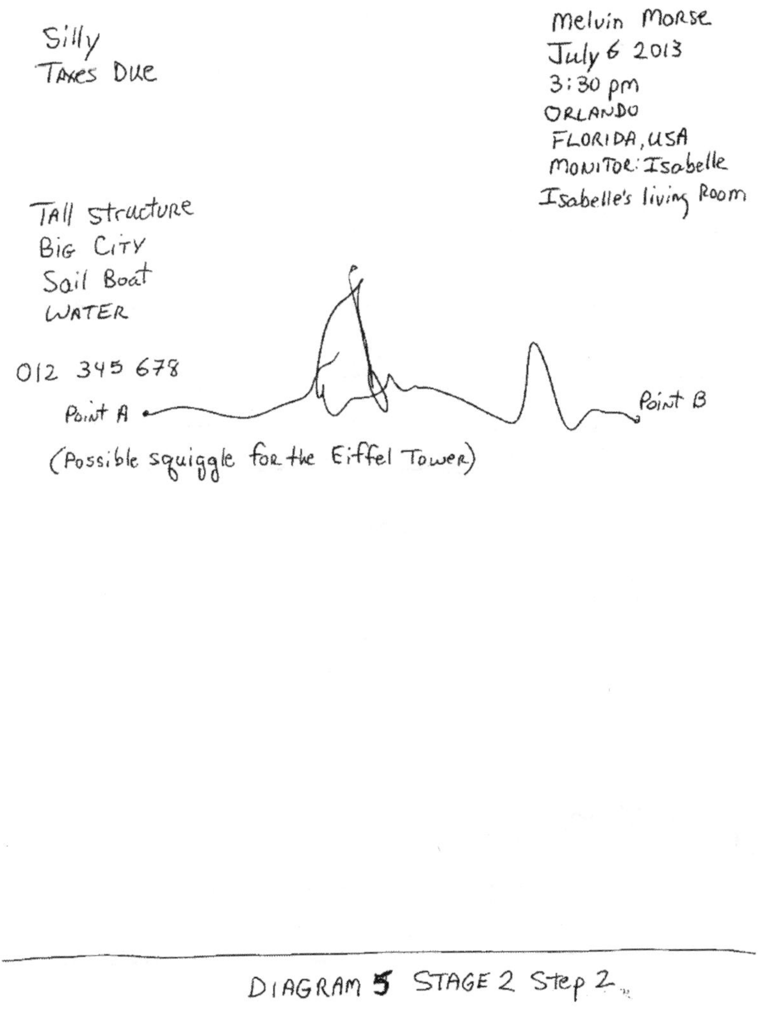

Silly
Taxes Due

Melvin Morse
July 6 2013
3:30 pm
ORLANDO
FLORIDA, USA
MONITOR: Isabelle
Isabelle's living Room

Tall Structure
Big City
Sail Boat
Water

012 345 678
Point A •   ~~~~~~~~~~~   • Point B
(Possible squiggle for the Eiffel Tower)

DIAGRAM 5 STAGE 2 Step 2

Diagram 5, Stage 2, Step 2

The hand, ideally, will jump with movement. The line is called a "Squiggle", but can be anything from a wiggly line, jagged pattern or absolutely straight line.

It should be a quick, non-thoughtful movement of the hand, guiding the pen from point A to point B.

We are energetic beings. Our brain and nervous system creates an electromagnetic field that is embedded in our bodies. It extends several feet outside the physical body.

Intention ~ merging

The brain's energetic field detects the unique energy signal of the remote site and causes the hand to move, creating the squiggle.

There are a multitude of possible squiggles representing the infinite possibilities of energetic signals from the site.

Any given remote site can cause different viewers to have

different squiggles. A given site can give the same viewer any number of different squiggles when taking the site address.

Ideally, there should be no analysis of the squiggle; it just is.

So what's the point

Step 2: Entering God's Reality: A Right Brain Exercise (Diagram 6, Stage 2, Step 2)

Step 2 is a right brain exercise. Successful completion of it indicates that the viewer has embraced egolessness and is in the right-brained mind set essential for Spiritual Sight.

"When egolessness arises, we can recognize it— a fresh moment, a clear perception of a smell, or a sight, or a sound, a feeling of opening to emotions or thoughts rather than a closing off into our narrow limited selves."

-- Pema Chodron

Step 2 involves describing and writing the journey of a subatomic particle along the line of the squiggle, from point A to point B. The point of view is from the perspective of the particle.

SPIRITUAL SIGHT – THE MANUAL

Silly
Taxes Due

MELVIN MORSE
July 6 2013
3:30 pm
ORLANDO
FLORIDA, USA
Monitor Isabelle
Isabelle's living Room

Tall Structure
Big City
Sail Boat
Water

012 345 678
Point A

Point B

(Possible Right brain Exercise in
Response to this Squiggle)

Curving over, curving down, curving under, diagonally up, curving over diagonally down, straight across, abruptly up, gentle curve, jagged turn down, plunging down, jagged up, curving over, curving under, straight up, jagged angled turn down, looping under, curving around, straight across, angled up, diagonal up, curving over, diagonal down, angled up, curving over, plunging down, curving under, curving over, curving under, gentle curve over, diagonal down, diagonal up, end.

DIAGRAM SIX: STAGE 2 STEP 2

Diagram 6, Stage 2, Step 2

Ordinarily, when we describe a journey, we describe it from a bird's eye point of view. We are objective observers describing the process.

For example, here is a typical description of a drive to the beach in a car. I might say, "I drove down the road, got on the highway, went around the Beltway, went over the mountains and arrived at the beach."

—Difference!

A child, in the same car, might say, "We went forward, then we curved around and around, then we went up and up, curved over the top and went down. We went on a long flat road and there was the beach."

The second description is a direct right brain description of exactly what the child in the car experienced. This is the mindset that is most conducive to successful Spiritual Sight. This is the perspective of someone who has left their ego behind and is directly experiencing reality completely in the here and now.

The viewer directly describes the movement of a

subatomic particle as it moves from point A to point B. The viewer will completely experience the totality of the energetic information signature of the site. Please note that although the line from point A to point B is called "the squiggle," it can be an entirely straight line. It is an impulsive movement of the hand.

Throughout step 2, the viewer says out loud and writes brief phrases such as "moving across," "moving up," "moving down," "making a sharp turn", "making a slow curve to the right," "spiraling down to the left," and so forth.

Jagged movements, slow curves, spirals, curving over and under, ups and downs, moving straight across and diagonally are all described as they are perceived as happening as the particle moves along the line from point A to point B.

The ride is not about the destination. Our experience here on earth is all about the spiritual journey, not the destination.

Sometimes taking the pen and retracing the line can help the viewer with this exercise in shifting to a right-brained childlike perspective of reality.

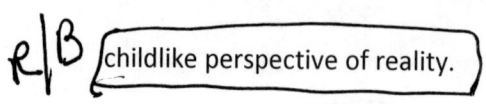

For example: If this is the squiggle:

A ————————————————————— B

The viewer might describe this as "moving across quickly."

However, the squiggle is a 2-dimensional representation of a 3-dimensional energy signal.

A ————————————————————— B

This could also be felt and described by the viewer as "moving up, sharp angle down, moving down, sharp angle up, curving over, slow slope down." This second example might be the energy signature of a mountain range. This looks the same as the first example. Both are 2 dimensional drawings of a 3 dimensional point of view. This is why a written description complements the visual representation of the squiggle.

These two examples illustrate the need to feel the

movement of the particle along the line instead of just describing what the viewer sees. It can be helpful for the viewer to pretend he or she is in a car moving along the line from point A to point B.

Step 3: A Brief Impression of the Site

After sensing the vibration of the site's energy signature, the viewer blurts out three quick words that describe the remote site. The monitor might prompt the viewer by saying, "Quick, three words to describe the site." The viewer's response should be immediate, without thought. If two words or four words tumble out, that is fine. The words should be written, as in Diagram 7, below the description of the squiggle.

For example, the Eiffel Tower's energy signal might cause a viewer to blurt, "Tall, busy, majestic." Another viewer, receiving he same energy signature, might blurt out, "Romance, passion, thin."

Silly
TAXES Due

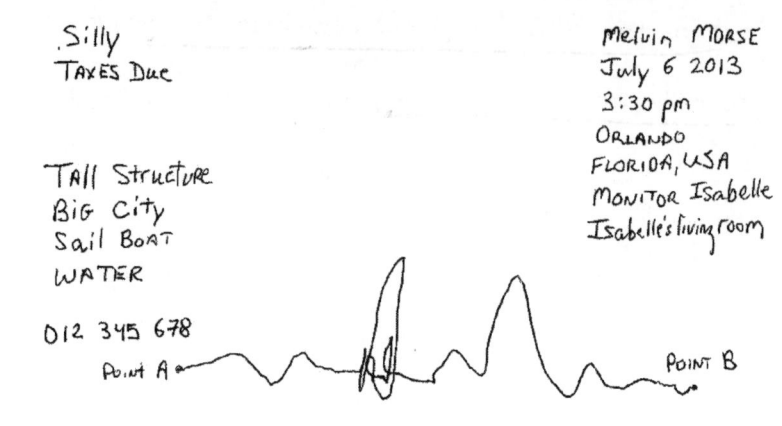

TAll Structure
BiG City
Sail BoAT
WATER

012 345 678

Melvin MORSE
July 6 2013
3:30 pm
ORLANDO
FLORIDA, USA
MONITOR Isabelle
Isabelle's living room

Point A ⸻∿∿⋀⋁∿⋀∿⸺ Point B

curving over, curving down, curving under, diagonally up, curving over, diagonally down, straight across, abruptly up, gentle curve, jagged turn down, plunging down, jagged up, curving over, curving under, straight up, jagged angled turn down, looping under, curving around, straight across, angled up, diagonal up, curving over, diagonal down, angled up, curving over, plunging down, curving under, curving over, curving under, gentle curve over, diagonal down, diagonal up, end

(Possible descriptive words of the Eiffel Tower)
ROMANCE, PASSION, thin

DIAGRAM 7   STAGE 2   Step 3

Diagram 7, Stage 2, Step 3

If the viewer unduly pauses or hesitates or makes obvious left brain analytic statements, the monitor might kindly suggest that the team start Stage 2 again, from the site address.

Examples of left brain analytic statements could include, "Hmmm, I'm thinking I am in a very romantic mood, I am thinking of someone I love." In this particular case, the romantic aspects of the Eiffel Tower might cause the viewer's analytic mind to shift to someone they love instead of continuing to access information from the remote site.

Spiritual Sight is a controlled process. The purpose of Stage 2 is to make a brief, powerful yet simple first description of the information streaming from the remote site.

One pitfall of Stage 2 Step 3 is that the viewer-monitor team can feel proud that they have correctly identified the remote site. Lengthy, detailed or even accurate descriptions of the site can create difficulties for the process. Similar to life itself, the purpose of Spiritual Sight is to grow spiritually from the journey. It is not about the destination, until the final site summary stage is experienced.

Step 4: Categorizing the Remote Site

At this point, the ego is intensely curious about the remote site. Research has shown that it is helpful to involve the ego, rather than completely shutting it out of the Spiritual Sight process.

The viewer is now asked to do one analytic task, to vaguely categorize the nature of the remote site. This helps to shape and guide the rest of the process.

The monitor prompts the viewer to categorize the site as biological, land, water, aerial, or man-made. After the viewer makes one response, the monitor then prompts the viewer again. "Is anything else present at the site, biological, land, water, aerial, or man-made?"

While learning the protocol of Spiritual Sight, it is best to use simple sites with no more than two major categories. For example, the Eiffel Tower would be land and man-made. A couple kissing at the top of the Eiffel Tower would be biological and man-made.

The category "biological" also includes people, one person, animals or one animal. It could also extend to the microscopic level (Ex: Remote Viewing a DNA double helix or an Ebola virus would be considered biological). The category "land" includes, for example, a mountain range or a desert. "Water" includes ponds, streams, waterfalls and oceans. "Aerial" includes a person parachuting in the air. A "manmade" could be anything from a building to a Zulu spear. A garden, although constructed by people, is considered land.

As in Step 3, the viewer blurts out the response to the monitor's prompting and writes the blurted word in the space indicated on Diagram 8, Stage 2, Step 4

Silly
TAXES Due

MELVIN MORSE
July 6 2013
3:30 PM
ORLANDO
FLORIDA, USA
MONITOR: Isabelle
Isabelle's living room

TALL STRUCTURE
BIG CITY
SAIL BOAT
WATER

012 345 678

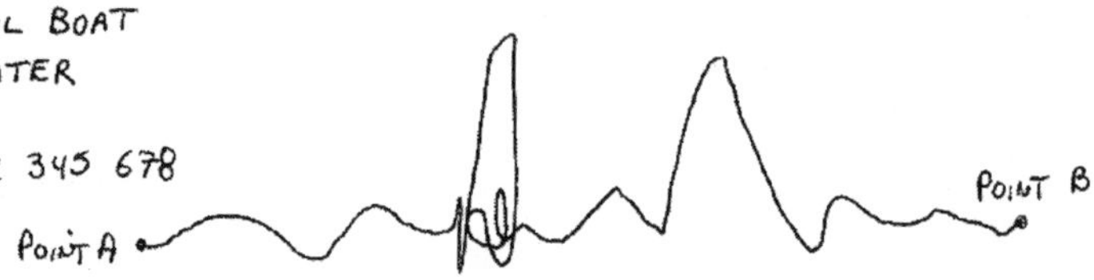

POINT A •   POINT B

curving over, curving down, curving under, diagonally up, curving over, diagonally down, straight across, abruptly up, gentle curve, jagged turn down, plunging down, jagged up, curving over, curving under, straight up, jagged angled turn down, looping under, curving around, straight across, angled up, diagonal up, curving over, diagonal down, angled up, curving over, plunging down, curving under, curving over, curving under, gentle curve over, diagonal down, diagonal up, end

ROMANCE, PASSION, THIN

(CATAGORIES FOR THE EIFFEL TOWER)
BIOLOGICAL, MAN-MADE, LAND

DIAGRAM 8   STAGE 2   STEP 4

Diagram 8, Stage 2, Step 4

It is not unusual for the blurted category to not accurately describe the site. This will become obvious to the viewer and monitor as the process continues to unfold. It can be easily corrected in the later stages. Valuable information and insight is gained even when the viewer and monitor work from a false category.

If the monitor knows the details of the remote site, and the viewer blurts an incorrect category, the monitor might elect to start Stage 2 over again.

The following is an example of a successful viewing from a false category. The remote site was a buffalo grazing in a National Park. The viewer blurted "water" and "land." He then went on to describe large round furry brown rocks surrounded by grass. The "rocks" were warm, made grunting noises, and were the size of small cars. No sensory impressions of "water" appeared and the viewer quickly lost interest in trying to describe them. This was a highly successful viewing and both monitor and viewer learned from it.

However, sometimes working from a false category can lead to the mind-brain inventing and embellishing sensory and descriptive information during the process. These are situations that the monitor can become aware of, and restart the process at Stage 2, Step 1.

Many viewer-monitor teams practice Stage 2 over and over until the viewer becomes highly accurate at quickly assessing the site category.

As in Step 3, if the viewer seems to be thinking too much, or the "blurt" becomes a prolonged pause or long sentence, the monitor might suggest starting Stage 2 over again from Step 1, the site address. Often, repeating the right brain exercise of Step 2 can help with the necessary immediacy of Steps 3 and 4.

For example, the viewer might say, "Hmmm, let me see, I think it is land." At that point the monitor might gently suggest repeating Stage 2 from Step 1.

The goal of Stage 2 is to sense the energetic signal from the remote site. This is a sudden non-conscious impulse. The viewer must be prepared to allow quick unbidden thoughts to arise spontaneously from the creator-God. The viewer-monitor team must have faith in the protocol and surrender to the process. The viewer speaks all thoughts out loud so that the monitor can help assess whether the thoughts come directly from the universal consciousness or are filtered and embellished too much by the mind-brain of the viewer. Some viewer-monitor teams prefer to postpone categorizing the site, as will be discussed.

Stage 3: Creating a Virtual Reality

"God wants us to have conversations with him."

--Neal Donald Walsch (Conversations with God)

Step by step, color by color, sound by sound, shape by shape, line by line, the viewer-monitor team now creates a virtual reality of the remote site.

The viewer says sensory impression of the colors, shapes, sounds, touches, smells, tastes and the general ambience of the site. They are stated out loud and listed as on diagram 9:

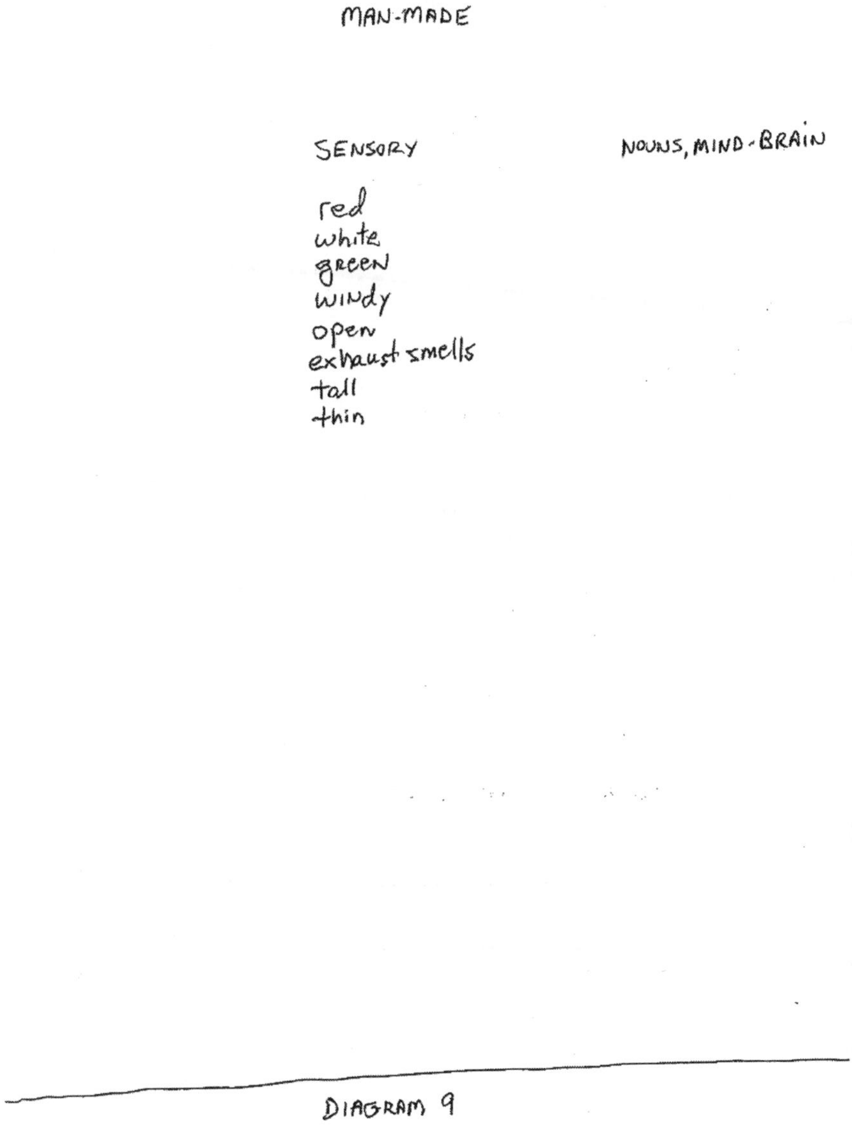

MAN-MADE

SENSORY

red
white
green
windy
open
exhaust smells
tall
thin

NOUNS, MIND-BRAIN

DIAGRAM 9

Diagram 9

First the team decides which category of the remote site to work on. The monitor will prompt the viewer as needed.

For Example:

1. What colors do you see?
2. What sounds do you hear?
3. Reach out and touch the site. What do you feel?
4. What odors do you smell?
5. What is the ambience of the site?
6. What shapes do you see? (Curved lines, horizontal lines, vertical lines, repetitive patterns)

The sensory impressions typically come as quick bursts of information spaced by pauses.

Other thoughts, emotions, and distorted impressions of the remote site will often intrude. They are also spoken out loud and recorded in the noun/mind-brain column on the right hand side of the page. See Diagram 10.

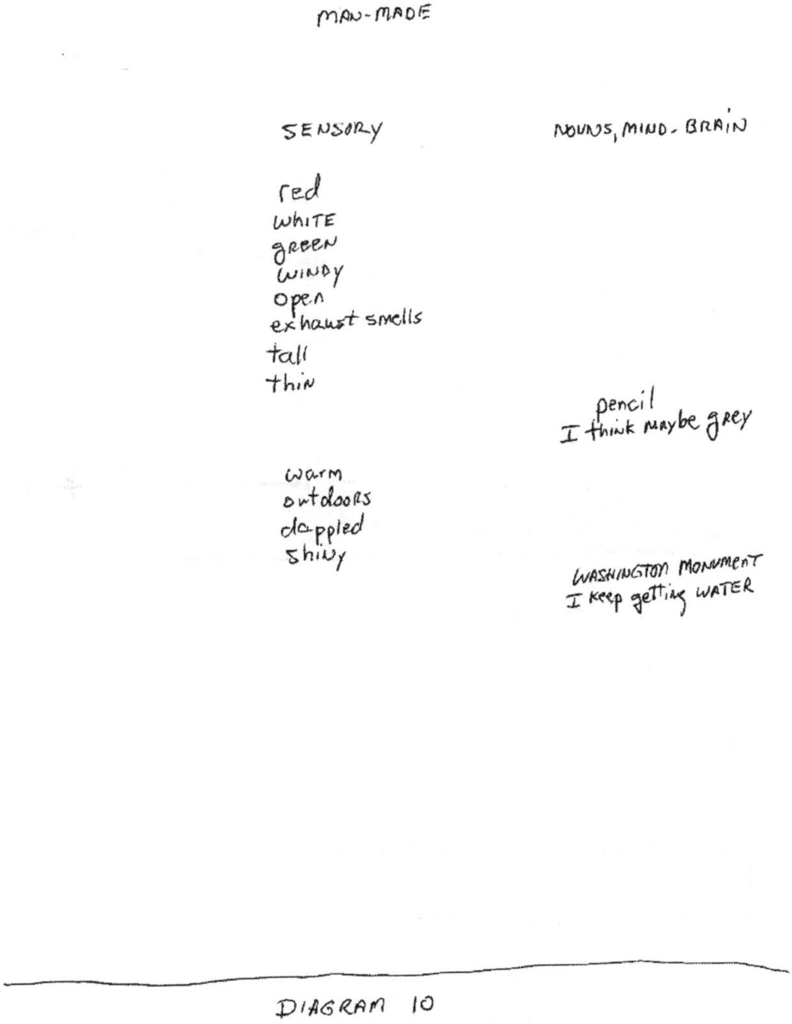

SPIRITUAL SIGHT – THE MANUAL

MAN-MADE

SENSORY   NOUNS, MIND-BRAIN

red
WHITE
green
WINDY
open
exhaust smells
tall
thin

                                                            pencil
                                         I think maybe grey

warm
outdoors
dappled
shiny

                                         WASHINGTON MONUMENT
                                         I keep getting WATER

DIAGRAM 10

Diagram 10

The monitor will help the viewer to sort and organize the information and place it in the appropriate column.

At this point, many monitor-viewer teams prefer to do Stage 2 Step 4, categorizing the site. They prefer to first let some sensory impressions come in and then categorize the site. This depends on the personality and spiritual style of the viewer. Many viewers do best with a slight left brain hint of what the nature of the remote site is all about. Others prefer to let some initial information from the site flood in, and then proceed to Stage 2 Step 4. Many advanced masters of Spiritual Sight never attempt to categorize the site at all.

For example one master of Spiritual Sight prefers to not limit his sessions by placing any categories on the experience. He was once given the remote site of a seagull in flight. He quickly became the seagull and experienced reality through the eyes of a seagull. Since a seagull doesn't know it is an animal, this result would have been difficult if he had first categorized the experience as biological.

For the novice, Spiritual Sight should first be learned precisely as outlined. As one becomes more experienced, the precise timing of Stage 2 Step 4 becomes flexible.

Furthermore, new categories will often pop out and can be explored as Stage 3 progresses. It is not unusual, for example, for the team to start exploring a category such as land. Then suddenly it will be obvious that a person is present.

During Stage 3 it may become obvious that a category was designated in Stage 2 Step 4 that does not exist at the remote site. When the viewer indicates a category during Stage 2 Step 4 that does not exist at the site, there will be very little sensory information about the category during Stage 3 and much of it will be obvious mind-brain inventions. The monitor can usually recognize the viewer is working from a mind-brain invented category.

If the category is actually present at the site, the flood of information will become richer in detail and spontaneous sketches will present themselves to the viewer.

If the monitor knows the identity of the remote site, he or she usually won't let the viewer work from a false category. Typically they will prompt the viewer to retake Stage 2 until the site is properly categorized

Stage 2 Step 4 can be retaken at any time during the process. The monitor simply has the viewer repeat and rewrite the site address. The viewer can then slowly count backwards from 15, taking slow deep breaths between each number. The monitor then asks, "Do you still feel (water) (the category in question) is present?"

If the viewer replies "yes," then a new sheet of paper is produced. The category is written at the top of the page (Diagram 9). Stage 3 is started again.

Ideally, sensory information from the site, such as shapes, colors, sounds, tactile impressions (smooth, rough, grainy, textured, etc.) and ambience will be listed in the center column.

Everything else is considered to be filtered through the

mind-brain and is listed in the right hand column. All nouns are ideally listed in the right hand column as by definition they come from the left brain. It is interesting that in the Old Testament, God gave Adam the task of naming the animals, plants and places of the Earth. This reinforces the concept that there are few nouns or names in God's view of reality.

The monitor takes charge of this purely organizational process. If questions arise during the protocol process, simply make a quick and non-judgmental decision. The process will be reviewed during the session summary.

It is most important that the information flows smoothly during Stage 3. The purpose of Stage 3 is to access information from the remote site. If nouns, for example, are placed in the center column, that can be corrected during the final summary. If there is confusion during the process, the team should take a short break. Highly accurate information typically floods in after short breaks.

At any time the monitor can have the viewer take a short

meditation pause, count backwards from 15, and/or retake the site address and write it down. The site address can be retaken at any time without redoing all of Stage 2.

As Stage 3 progresses, the sensory information will become more complex. Images such as "patterned," "dimpled," "ridged" will appear. There will be a sense of density, volume and size. The monitor can prompt the viewer with questions such as, "Is the manmade dense or hollow?" "What size are the animals, small, medium or large?" The monitor can ask questions such as, "Are you indoors or outdoors?" and "Is there one person, two people or many people?"

The team can take breaks and change categories whenever either team member wants to explore a different category.

Curiosity is essential, in both the monitor and viewer, in exploring the remote site.

Sometimes the ego of the viewer will override the viewing and impose a firm fixed opinion about the remote site. For example, while attempting to view the Eiffel Tower, the viewer might have persistent images of the Seattle Space Needle. Or, the viewer might have persistent visual images of the correct remote site, the Eiffel Tower. Either situation can create problems for the viewing.

No effort should be made to assess if the recurrent persistent image is correct or not. Spiritual Sight should be free from judgment or analysis. When the viewing process Is complete and feedback given, then the viewer and monitor can properly assess the accuracy of images that come up during the viewing.

Spiritual patience is learned by practicing Spiritual Sight. In life, we often do not understand the spiritual significance of events until time has passed. There is a Native American story, often told, about an American Native who dreams of a son caring for him in his old age. His son is crippled fighting a bear. The man is devastated. Then a rival tribe raids the settlement and kills all the young men. The man's son is spared because of his disability. This story illustrates the difficulty in assessing even our most serious challenges, from a greater spiritual point of view.

When nouns and specific images such as "Space Needle" come to the viewer during the Spiritual Sight process, they are not judged as "right" or "wrong." They are simply set aside, in the right hand column of the paper (Diagram 11). If the same image occurs again and again, the monitor can ask the viewer what specific sensory impressions are triggering the recurrent image.

For example, if the viewer keeps reporting seeing the Seattle Space Needle, then space needle is written on the right hand side of the paper. The monitor asks the viewer to then list the sensory impression he or she has of the Space Needle. The viewer lists them in the center column, directly below the level of the words "Space Needle." (Diagram 2) Those sensory impressions might be "tall, thin, landmark, windy, outdoors, open, vast space." The monitor carefully documents that these impression came from the recurrent image of the Space Needle, in the monitor's notes of the viewing.

This is an example of data mining a recurrent noun or visual image.

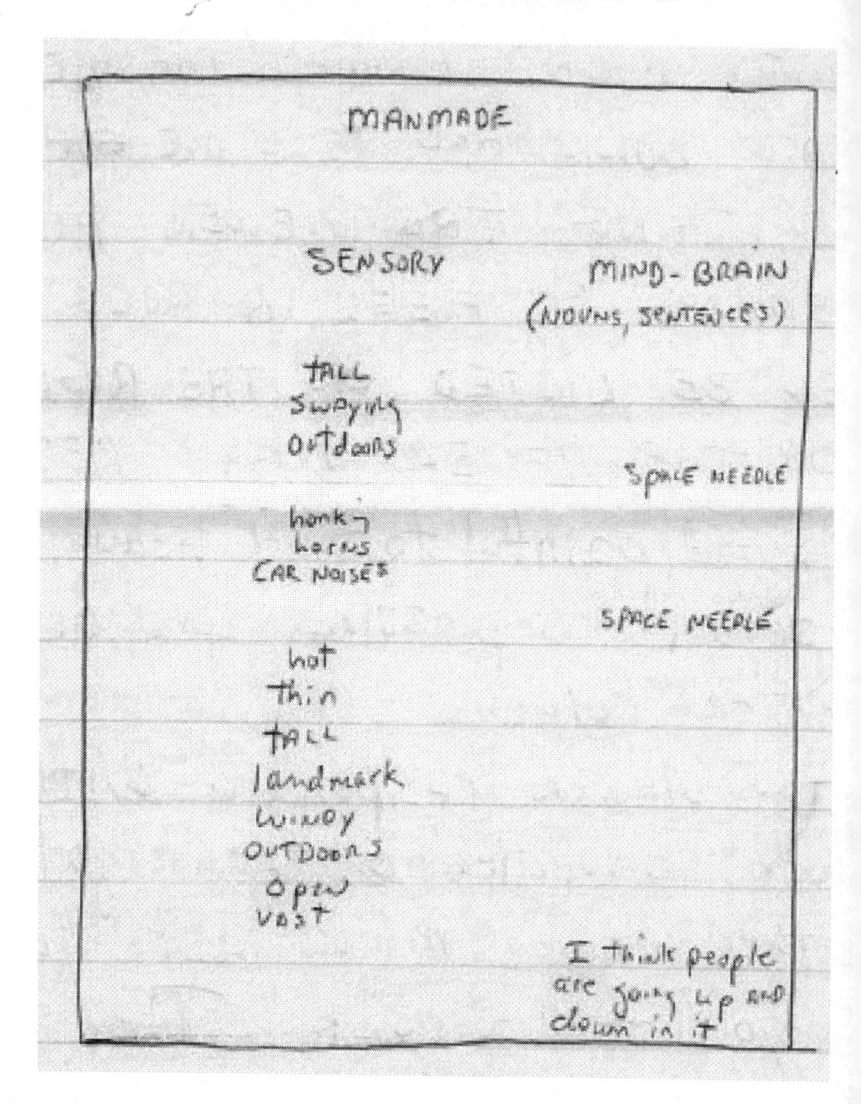

```
                MANMADE

         SENSORY           MIND-BRAIN
                          (NOUNS, SENTENCES)
           tall
           swaying
           outdoors
                            SPACE NEEDLE
           honky
           horns
           CAR NOISES
                            SPACE NEEDLE
           hot
           thin
           tall
           landmark
           windy
           outdoors
           open
           vast
                       I think people
                       are going up and
                       down in it
```

Diagram 11

Think of Stage 3 as similar to an artist creating a highly detailed and realistic drawing. First there will be simple lines, shapes and colors. As more information about the picture is added, there will be perceptions of size, complex shapes such as cubes and cylinders, shades of light, and density. Patterns such as ridges, grooves and dapples will appear. Complex perception such as reflective surfaces and semi-transparent objects will be present. This is the same process of building a virtual reality with Spiritual Sight. Remember that the spiritual information is being plugged into the same mind-brain system that an artist uses in painting a realistic picture.

The information in the center column is the same information the viewer or an artist on location senses at the site.

The monitor might prompt the viewer by saying, "<u>Reach down and tell me what you feel, if anything.</u>" The viewer might respond, saying, "I feel a rock." "Rock" would then be listed on the right hand column. Or, the viewer might respond and say, "Hard, jagged, painful to touch, heavy, dense." These are ensory impressions and are listed in the center column.

If the viewer responded with "rock," after "rock" is written on the right hand column, the monitor might ask, "What do you feel when you feel a rock?" Then the viewer might respond with, "Hard, jagged, painful to touch, heavy, dense." These would be listed in the center column, under the level of the word "rock." The monitor would separately note that these sensories were brought out by data mining the word "rock."

The viewer-monitor team can practice for Stage 3 by describing ordinary reality. For example, they can take a drinking glass. The monitor can prompt, "What do you feel?" The viewer might reply, "Firm, curved surface, cool, hard."

The monitor might ask, "What shapes do you see?" The viewer might reply, "I see a cylinder and a circle." The team could then discuss that the viewer typically does not actually see a circle. Usually the viewer sees several curved lines and mentally constructs a circle, from prior knowledge of drinking glasses.

"I see a circle" is valuable information. During a session, it would be properly placed on the right hand side of the page. It is not "wrong" information. It is a blend of sensory information (the semi-circular curved lines) and mind-brain analysis coupled with memories of circular-shaped drinking glasses.

The monitor might prompt the viewer by saying, "What did you see that made you think of a circle?" The viewer might respond with, "I saw two curved lines." These would be listed in the center column.

"Sour milk" is also a possibly sensory impression from a drinking glass. "Sour smell" would be listed in the central column. "Milk" is a noun and would be listed on the right hand column. The monitor can assist in the organization of the words to the various columns.

These exercises help the viewer to sort out direct sensory impressions from the remote site, and mind-brain analysis of those same sensory impressions. This is an important process in energetic healing and spiritual inspiration. A Reiki therapist once told me she had difficulties sorting, "My stuff from the client's stuff. Yet that is what I need to do to be a successful Reiki therapist." There are many examples, unfortunately, of people who distort communications from God with their own mind-brain analysis, in harmful and destructive ways. Spiritual Sight teaches the basic process of recognizing and distinguishing spiritual information from our own "stuff" created by our unique mind-brains.

The viewer-monitor team should spend considerable time practicing Stage 3 on known landscapes, water scenes, man-made buildings and objects, people and animals so that actual Spiritual Sight viewings flow smoothly.

It should now be obvious why the viewer should strive to say all thoughts out loud, no matter how fleeting, inconsequential or absurd. This will assist the monitor in the task of sorting and organizing the incoming information from the remote site.

The viewer-monitor team should take frequent 30 second

to 5 minute breaks. Laughter and silly behavior will often break up the tension of a difficult viewing. One master of Spiritual Sight squawks like a chicken and barks like a dog during breaks.

After a break, it is often helpful for the monitor to repeat the site address to the viewer. The viewer says it out loud and writes it down. Often a brief simple meditation such as breathing while counting backwards can be helpful.

The most important priority is for the viewer to continue the flow of information. The monitor can improvise notes if the information becomes confusing, chaotic, or out of protocol. It is more important that the viewer continue to simply blurt out all ideas, thoughts, feeling and sensory impressions without any effort to restrict, analyze or judge the information.

For example, while viewing the Eiffel Tower, the viewer might think, "I think I see a red, white and blue flag." Then, "Oops, that's a noun. I'm not supposed to think about nouns, it must not be real." Often such thoughts are suppressed. In this case, it might represent the French flag, an important piece of information directly from the signal line of the Eiffel Tower. Ideally, "red, white and blue flag" would be expressed and documented on the right hand side of the paper.

Another common example is the perception of a sensory impression that doesn't fit in with the other sensories. For example, while viewing the Eiffel Tower and getting sensories consistent with the Tower, the viewer might hear an airplane engine. He or she might suppress it. Yet at the time of the viewing a small plane might be flying over the Eiffel Tower. Ideally this should be said out loud, "Airplane noise" and listed in the center column.

Sometimes unexpressed thoughts will distort the sensory data. For example, the viewer might think, "I think it's the Seattle Space Needle. Oops, I'm not supposed to guess the remote site. I better not think that." The viewer might not say this out loud, resulting in the monitor being unaware that the viewer is thinking, "Space Needle."

The viewer's ego, in its relentless desire to be "right,"

might then invent sensory impressions to match the Seattle Space Needle. For example, the viewer might "hear" water sounds as the Space Needle is near water, or the sounds of the amusement park at the base of the Space Needle.

The monitor can help to filter out these false impressions, but only if the viewer discloses the image of the Space Needle. This is but one example of why the viewer should say all thoughts out loud.

If the viewer discloses the thought, "Space Needle," it is then written in the right-hand column. The monitor can now prompt the viewer by saying, "What are the sensory impressions of the Space Needle that apply here?" Now the viewer's ego can get involved in a positive way and say, for example, "Tall, thin, in a big city, traffic sounds," as it won't have the urge to invent false impressions.

These sensories, which fit both the Space Needle and the actual target, the Eiffel Tower, are written in the center column.

These exercises help the viewer's spiritual mind and ego to learn to work together in the greater task of appreciation of the creator-God within us. It is generally considered that the ego interferes with spiritual insights. Spiritual Sight teaches the ego to work in harmony with the egoless mind that connects us to the divine.

Although the ego can be harnessed in Spiritual Sight, in general the monitor tries to take up as much of the viewer's ego functions as possible. The monitor is responsible for having the team take regular breaks to assess the flow and documentation of information. Together they mutually decide which parts of the site they want to explore if there is more than one category of information, for example, land and a manmade. Together they can decide what category to explore and the monitor will prepare a sheet of paper as in diagram 12:

SPIRITUAL SIGHT – THE MANUAL

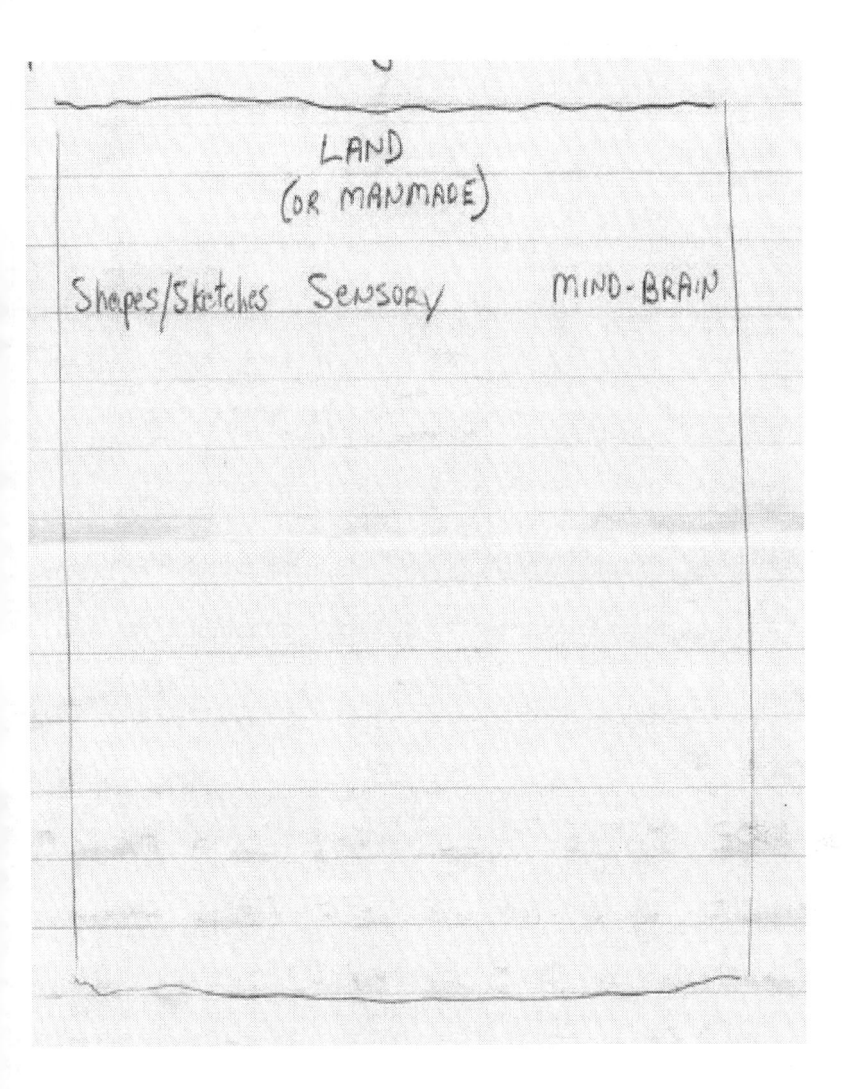

LAND
(OR MANMADE)

Shapes/Sketches   Sensory   MIND-BRAIN

Diagram 12

The center column is for the sensory information from the site. The right-hand column is for all nouns and sentence fragments (such as "I think it's green," or "uh, hmmm, green," and other mind-brain derived information. As shapes and brief sketches present themselves, they are placed in the left-hand column.

As the viewer enters information on the paper, it should be sequentially charted flowing from the top to the bottom, regardless of which column it is placed in. This is to keep track of the proper time sequence of the flow of information.

For example: Diagram 13

SPIRITUAL SIGHT – THE MANUAL

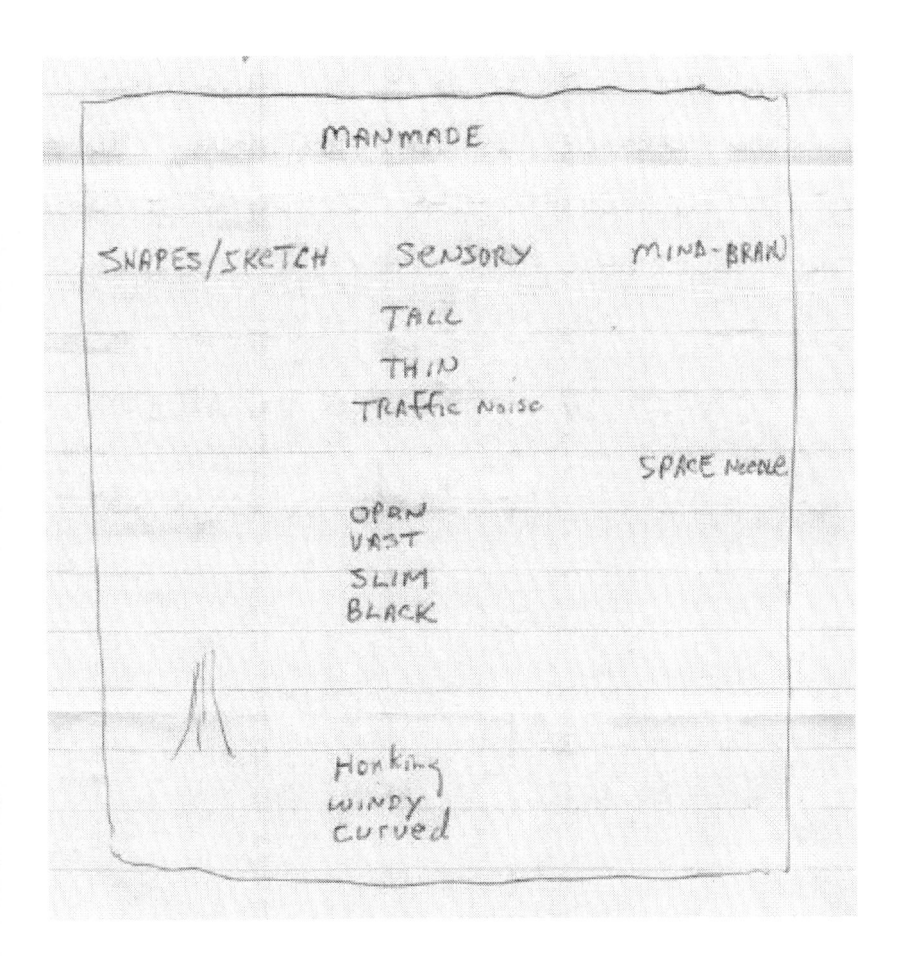

```
                    MANMADE

SHAPES/SKETCH     SENSORY         MIND-BRAIN
                  TALL
                  THIN
                  TRAffic Noise
                                  SPACE NEEDLE
                  OPEN
                  VAST
                  SLIM
                  BLACK


                  Honking
                  Windy
                  Curved
```

Diagram 13

Be patient. Let the data from the remote site accumulate. After enough information is received, vague shapes and quick sketches will spontaneously emerge to the viewer's consciousness. The blank areas of the virtual reality are slowly, tediously being filled in. Quickly draw these images in the left hand column.

The Emotional Reaction to the Site

We know more than we think we know. If you want to try to reclaim some of this deeper knowledge, I suggest that you start with emotion, which to me seems to reside at the interface between that part of self that is accessible to awareness, and that part which is not.

--Herbert Benson, *The Relaxation Response*

At some point, the viewer will have an emotional response to the remote site. Recognizing this emotional reaction to the remote site is an important step prior to making site contact and sketching the site. This typically heralds the end of Stage 3 and the start of Stage 4.

If the site is a city, for example, and the viewer loves cities, there may be an emotional response of fun and adventure. If cities are too noisy and dirty for a viewer's sensibilities, the emotional response might be one of anxiety and distaste.

Human emotion becomes part of our perception of reality, even before we are directly conscious of whatever it is that we are perceiving. Psychologists have shown that humans even react emotionally to nonsense words, illustrating how universal an emotional response to perception is. For example, for English-speaking subjects, "ju valuma" is pleasing to the ear, whereas "chakaka" is despised.

Dr Raymond Moody, Ph.D. reports in his unpublished book "The Secret World of Nonsense" more than 30 different types of nonsensical words or expressions. He and Lisa Smartt M.A. are studying the final words of the dying in a project called The Final Words Project. In this study, they have already preliminarily found that nonsensical words blurted by the dying a few days before their passing are often time fully charged of emotional meaning and utterly "God – Creative Source" information infused.

We similarly have an unconscious emotional reaction to the virtual reality we create with Spiritual Sight. This emotional response is the key to untapping a vast reservoir of unconscious manifestations of information from the remote site.

This emotional reaction signals the end of Stage 3 and the beginning of Stage 4. It is documented in the center column of the page that the team is working on. After it is recorded, a fresh sheet of paper should be labeled Stage 4.

If the viewer doesn't spontaneously have an emotional response to the site, the monitor can prompt it by saying, "What emotions, if any, do you feel about the site." The timing of such a prompt is part of the art of being a monitor.

It could be difficult sometimes reporting the emotions felt at the site and by the site. Eben Alexander, author of "Proof of Heaven" says that it is almost impossible to find words to define what is felt in the "God-creative source" state, that there is no language appropriate for that because it is beyond our realm of comprehension.

But the viewer has to do his or her best to find the best attributes to describe the target he or she is viewing, digging into his or her most interpersonal relationship with the Universe. That is when experiencing nonsense emotional reaction or feeling the need of blurting nonsensical or inconsequential words is a critical part of any viewing.

Stage 4: Site Contact

We are forever comparing the world perceived by our senses with the world created with a model in our minds. When the match is good, we accept this as reality.

--James Lovelock

SPIRITUAL SIGHT – THE MANUAL

The viewer makes firm contact with the remote site in Stage 4. The signal line is now very clear.

On a blank sheet of paper, the monitor prompts the viewer to make a fast spontaneous sketch of the site. The hand should move almost automatically. Care should be taken that the viewer not *draw*, but quickly sketch. There should ideally be no thought to the process. There may be one sketch or a series of sketches. The monitor supplies as many pieces of paper as needed, and labels them appropriately.

Most likely, the viewer will not be able to organize the sketches into a recognizable picture. This is often the monitor's job.

Split brain research demonstrates that the left brain recognizes patterns and the right brain is detail oriented.

For example, research subjects are given a picture of the letter A composed of Z's as pixels:

figure 1

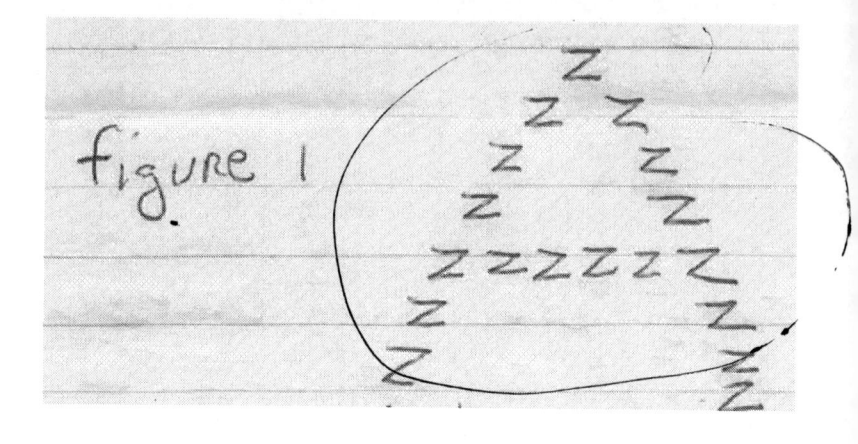

```
        Z
      Z   Z
    Z       Z
  Z           Z
    ZZZZZZZ
  Z           Z
Z               Z
                Z
```

The left brain, the ego, working alone, sees this as a simple A shape and doesn't see the Z's.

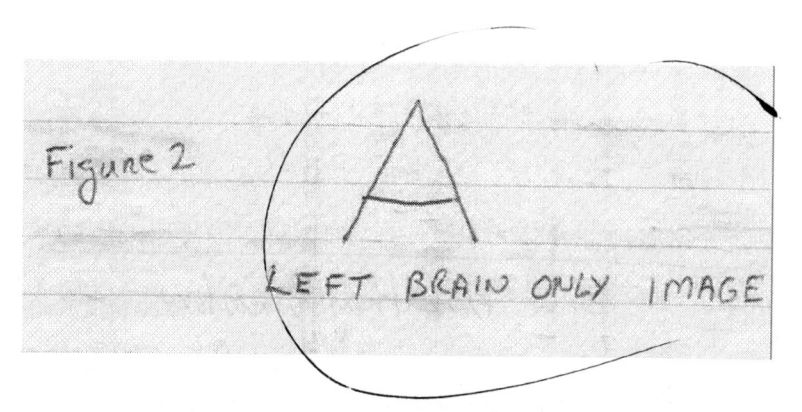

Figure 2

A

LEFT BRAIN ONLY IMAGE

The right brain, (the spiritual brain) does not see the pattern at all, but only sees the Z subunits. It will draw a big pile of Z's when shown figure 1.

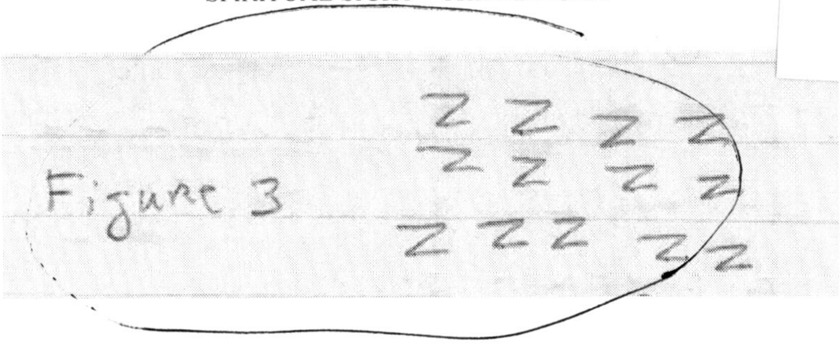
Figure 3

• This concept is further illustrated when researchers ask the right brain to draw a picture of a clock.

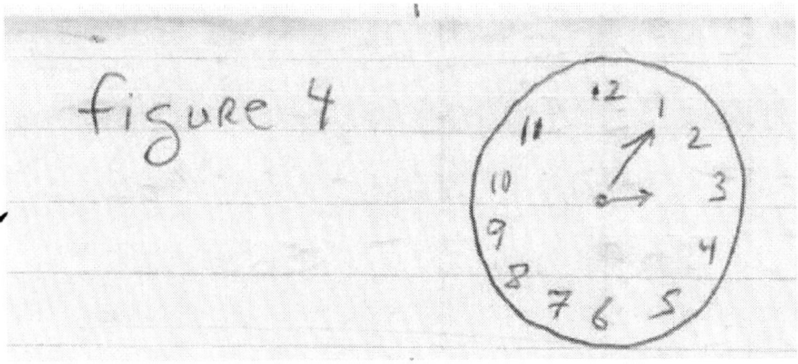
figure 4
12
1
2
3
4
5
6
7
8
9
10
11

Both brains working together.

The right brain will draw the following picture, or something similar:

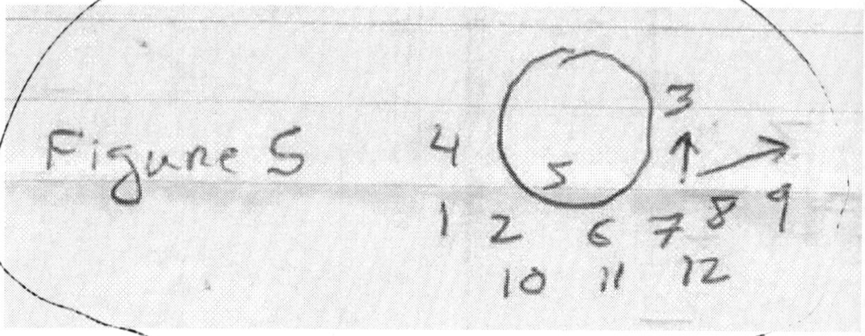
Figure 5
4
3
5
1 2 6 7 8 9
10 11 12

Right brain only clock.

It is the right brain that accesses information from the remote site. So the sketches in Stage 4 will resemble the pictures in Figure 3 and Figure 5. All the pieces will be present, but they may be rotated or not assembled into a recognizable picture.

The viewer should not attempt to organize the sketches nor label or name the remote site. The viewer's job is to simply access and sketch the information however it presents to the viewer's mind-brain.

After the initial sketches are made, the team can take a break. Together they can plan further exploration of the sketches of the site. Sensory impressions of the sketches can be written directly next to the sketch.

Curiosity is vital to successful Spiritual Sight. The team will wonder about various parts of the sketches. Areas can be marked with numbers. The monitor can then ask the viewer to report specific sights, sounds, textures and tastes of specifically labeled areas.

The monitor can and should move the viewer around the site. For example, the monitor might say, "Move 500 feet above the site, look down and tell me what you see. Sketch it," or "Move 10 feet in front of the manmade and describe," or "Reach down to the ground, if any, and describe what you feel," or "Move to the area labeled '1' and describe." These are but a few possible prompts by the monitor, as curiosity about the site dictates. (Diagram 14, Stage 4)

STAGE FOUR
(Possible Sketches of a Tower)

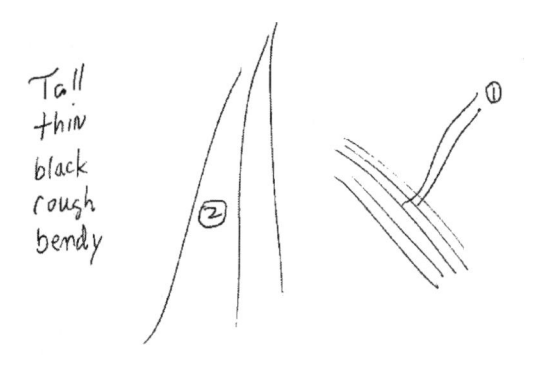

Tall
thin
black
rough
bendy

① HARD POINTY, PAINFUL, WARM, WINDY, OUTSIDE

Communication Tower
Point 1 is a Top

② Open, diagonal lines, black, firm, traffic sounds, humming, swooshing

DIAGRAM 14 STAGE 4

Diagram 14, Stage 4

Such movements around the site should be made (slowly)

and patiently. The monitor should give the viewer plenty of time and be careful not to rush the process.

The monitor should prompt the viewer, and not ask questions. If the monitor asks, "Do you want to move 500 feet above the site?" the viewer will have to think about answering and will break out of the trance. The team should take breaks to discuss how to explore the site. Then the monitor should prompt the viewer in a relaxed and straight-forward manner.

If the viewer resists the monitor's prompts, the monitor should immediately retract the prompt. There may be sound psychic reasons to avoid a given area of a site.

All efforts by the viewer to name or otherwise label the site should be duly noted on the right-hand side of the paper. They often are very accurate by Stage 4. However too much emphasis on them can dampen the free flow of information from the site. They should be documented and the team should take a break. Typically new sketches and a flood of highly accurate new information will follow.

Beware of ego overdrive. This occurs when the viewer becomes preoccupied with one particular idea of what is the remote site. Often this conviction is correct. More commonly the viewer seizes on a solution which is strikingly similar to the actual remote site. For example, the viewer might visualize a surfer surfing a wave, whereas the remote site is actually a man on a sailboard surfing a wave.

The purpose of Spiritual Sight is to listen to the voice of the universe and create a virtual reality from the information contained in that view. Tibetan Buddhists call this "The View." The View is both the sensory perception of this reality and the silent wisdom of the egoless mind. It is the totality of consciousness: The active ego-driven mind and the silent spiritual consciousness.

When the viewer becomes convinced he or she has understood the remote site, then no more information comes from the spiritual mind, or that information becomes distorted by the viewer's mind-brain.

Spiritual Sight is a spiritual training exercise designed to assist us in identifying the still quiet voice of the wisdom within each one of us. Much harm has been done by well-intentioned persons who hear yet distort the voice of the creator-god.

It takes patience and mental discipline to simply listen to the creative source of wisdom in our lives. We must resist the natural urge to interpret this still quiet voice, instead of surrendering to it.

The Jewish religion prohibits making statues of God, or even giving God a name. This is to remind us that such efforts distort and limit God's true nature.

When ego overdrive occurs, the team should take a break. The viewer can do a brief meditation, then retake the site address. Often the entire second stage should be repeated. There are other specific exercises that help to return the viewer to the signal line, that are part of more advanced manuals.

o Ask Melvin

Well-disciplined masters of Spiritual Sight are rarely certain that they understand the true nature of the remote site until the process is complete and feedback given.

The viewer and monitor, with practice, will learn to be confident that they are on the signal line. This mental experience is akin to knowing one is on God's path but being unaware of where it is going. Hence the expression, "Let go, Let God." This is a unique experience for each individual and can be learned through direct experience.

There is a confidence and serene joy in knowing one has found his or her individual unique signal line in life. It can comfort one through the most painful trials and tribulations. It does not involve having certainty as to what will be a given outcome in one's life, only that one is on God's path.

Sometimes the information from the remote site will simply seem to disintegrate and vanish. This may mean that site contact was not made. If this occurs, simply take a break or end the session altogether. The viewer can retake the site address, retake Stage 2, or simply try again at a future time.

When site contact is made, typically the information from the site will become more and more complex. New people, animals, manmade elements and places may appear. There will be continued bursts of information. This often means the viewer is ready for the advanced stage, which involves entering the virtual reality and interacting with the site.

Until the viewer-monitor team has mastered the first four stages, they should end the session after Stage 4. Typically, as site contact is made, there is a sense of completion with an anticipation of more to come. This is the perfect time to end Stage 4.

Every viewer-monitor team will progress at a different rate. Usually after the team has viewed a remote site successfully several dozen times through Stage 4, they are ready to progress to a virtual encounter with the site.

If the team is not ready for advanced stages, yet the viewer starts to talk with people or physically interact with the site, the monitor should gently and slowly bring the session to a close. There are specialized tools for use at the advanced stages. It is best to make site contact and have a successful Stage 4 experience and then bring the session to a close. Then get advanced training for the advance stages.

Session Summary

"Through spiritual training we are brought to re-awaken to our true nature, the joy and freedom of what we truly are... the wisdom that realizes egolessness. In this time of violence and disintegration, spiritual vision is not an elitist luxury but vital to our survival."

--Sogyal Rinpoche

At the end of Stage 4, a narrative summary complete with representative sketches should be compiled. It should end with the statement, "End session" and the time of completion.

The monitor takes the lead in creating the summary. It should consist of the sensory information in the center column, and the sketches. The mind-brain information in the right-hand column is compiled in a separate section at the end.

As the monitor and viewer review the session, the viewer can add information or remove impressions that no longer seem pertinent. Research has shown that the viewer retains site contact through the end of the session summary. The viewer may feel that he or she is second guessing the viewing process. Learning which second guesses are accurate and which ones led to the removal of accurate information is an important part of the spiritual training process. For most individuals, second guessings are typically inaccurate and lead to the removal of accurate information. However some second impressions are uncannily accurate and helpful.

If the site is the Eiffel Tower, a site summary might be as follows: "The site is land and a manmade. The manmade is tall, black, hatched lines, outside, open air, swaying with multiple horizontal and diagonal lines. It is metallic, smells sweaty. There are many people, excited, bustling, wandering, with a touristy feel to the place. The land is in a large city, traffic noises, flat, hard surface, noisy. The emotional impression for the viewer is romantic and patriotic."

There would be a few representative sketches.

The mind-brain information would be summarized as follows: "The site reminded the viewer of the Seattle Space Needle, the Arc de Triumph, and Baltimore's Shot Tower. The viewer had recurrent images of elevators throughout the viewing."

A typical site summary is longer than the above, usually one complete side of an 8x11 sheet of paper.

Feedback

"The road to wisdom? Well, it's plain and simple to express. Err, and err, and err again, but less and less and less."

--Bo Lazloff

After the site summary is complete, the viewer is then taken to the remote site or shown photographs. The summary is compared to the actual site.

Often the viewer will access information not visible on one photograph, so multiple photographs are helpful.

The team should carefully review the site summary to differentiate accurate information from distorted and inaccurate information. In this fashion the viewer or the viewer-monitor team (if the monitor is unaware of the site during the viewing) can fine tune intuitive skills. There is a unique mental experience to intuition, which can be appreciated with the feedback process. One purpose of the Spiritual Sight protocol is to learn, in a controlled manner, what that unique experience is like for a given individual.

In this way the team can learn to appreciate the faint ding of God's presence in our lives.

Spiritual Sight, Why?

"My brain is only a receiver, in the Universe there is a core from which we obtain knowledge, strength and inspiration. I have not penetrated into the secrets of this core, but I know that it exists."

— Nikola Tesla

Spiritual Sight has practical applications, from finding missing children to energetic healing. These are advanced applications.

Spiritual Sight's highest purpose is to teach us how to contact that infinite reservoir of God's love and wisdom that exists in each one of us.

"When God's love rises as a wave, it washes away the sins of a whole life in a moment, for the law has no power to stand before love. The stream of life sweeps it away."

--Hazrat Inayat Khan

ABOUT THE AUTHORS

MELVIN L. MORSE, M.D.

Melvin Morse graduated with academic honors from the George Washington University School of Medicine. He trained at Seattle Children's Hospital and was an associate professor of pediatrics at the University of Washington for 20 years. He was selected as one of the nation's best pediatricians by his peers from 1997 through 2004. Dr. Morse was a pioneer in Near Death Research. His research has been featured in documentaries in the U.S. and other countries. He has appeared on numerous television and radio shows, including 20/20, The Oprah Winfrey Show, The Turning Point, The Tom Snyder Show, the Larry King Show, Good Morning America, Dateline, and Unsolved Mysteries, and has been the subject of lengthy profiles in the Seattle Times, Tacoma News Tribune, and the Los Angeles Times.

He has numerous scientific publications on death and dying, including The Lancet and the American Medical Association's Pediatric Journal. He has also published scientific articles on energetic healing and remote viewing.

Morse's first book, *Closer to the Light*, was an international best seller and is published in 38 countries and 19 languages. It explored the near death experiences of children.

His best-selling second book, *Transformed by the Light*, is a long term follow up of these children as adults, and documents the physical and psychological transformations resulting from near death experiences.

His third book, *Parting Visions*, documents the entire range of spiritual visions associated with death and dying, including premonitions of death and after death visitations. It focuses on how we can use these experiences to help us to understand death, grief, and the often overlooked spiritual miracles in everyday life.

His fourth book, "Where God Lives: Paranormal Science and How Our Brains Are Connected To The Universe" discusses the "God Spot" that we all have as part of the anatomy of our brains. This book details Dr. Morse's theory that we are all spiritual beings using our brains and bodies to have a human experience.

Dr. Morse is trained by Lyn Buchanan and Paul Smith PhD in the art of Controlled Remote Viewing. He has presented at the International Remote Viewing Association (IRVA) multiple times over the past 20 years. He has also been trained in remote viewing by Stephan Schwartz.

ISABELLE A. CHAUFFETON SAAVEDRA

Isabelle Chauffeton Saavedra studied mathematics and physics in France, her home country, and was an entrepreneur creating and managing businesses in three different continents for 18 years.

Armed with a passion for astronomy since her childhood and college years she has used her knowledge and experience to envision theories about how we as humans are all connected within our Universe(s).

Realizing that our brains have a capability to connect at a much deeper level than just our first five senses, Isabelle Chauffeton Saavedra started to experiment early on with ESP.

Today, after years of practice refining her technique and methodology, Isabelle Chauffeton Saavedra has become a professional psychic medium who reconnects people through different levels of Consciousness while tackling the most important questions about our presence in the Universe(s).

Setting herself apart from an often time sensationalized media driven industry, Isabelle Chauffeton Saavedra strives to promote an ethical and respectable form of psychic experimentalism.

Her double blind technique sets her apart from most psychic mediums. Isabelle Chauffeton Saavedra does all her readings at a distance without knowing, or seeing or hearing her sitters (and vice versa). Her sitters do not know when their readings are done within a period of 14 days from the day of confirmation; thus creating a double-blind setting which allows all information to flow without restrictions or risks of pollution by outside trigger behaviors such as body language of the sitters or facial expressions, or immediate feedback. Feedback is usually discussed in a lengthy manner post reading with the sitters at their convenience.

Her deep interest in understanding how consciousness and quantum physics, two subjects that seem diametrically opposed, can be so very much closely intertwined takes her clients on logical yet emotional new paths of seeing how we are all connected.

In her first book, *"God Consciousness, the Journey of a Science Driven Psychic medium"*, Mrs. Chauffeton Saavedra takes her readers through the meanders of our Consciousness. While proposing scientific explanations to the many questions arising from our quest in understanding our place in our Universe(s), she recalls how her own life triggered her thirst for knowledge.

She shares her passion with her husband and her two children.

Her second passion is music and singing. Writing songs is also an act of connecting with Consciousness and she particularly loves the exercise.

She keeps a Facebook page under her name and can be found on her website for informational blogging and private readings.

www.survivalofconsciousness.com

Or email at isabelle@survivalofconsciousness.com

Melvin - Do you still need/use a monitor
- Have you tried med.?
- Protocols of Brazilian spiritists

p. 54 - Remain convinced they're wrong
o Explain p. 55
o Did you come up w/ the term Spiritual Sight

Share p. 57 - That's it!

Site address! = SFFC
p. 114 - why?

Cosmometry

Lynn Lew's synchronicity

---

o Great class ex. for objectivity
p. 122

o Ask Melvin - advanced manuals?
(See p. 145

☆° Direct hit
    Site Contact   } Apply to
    Miss   mediumship
                                      5 + 6

Bill Harvey - Mind Magic

– Site Address = SFIC

⑥   p. 59   Embracing Uncertainty

Finding the Signal Line'

How we "know" / How knowing happens
1. Past experience. "This is my name"
2. A realm of intuitive knowledge
Intuition = God's language

The # is the site address for the entire energetic signal + bundled info –

☆☆ What if we give each session a
⟶ Code/# that holds their intention for the site?!

Annaliese Frisk - participate in Morse's study! (Schwartz p.156 synch.)

- Morse - The God Spot
- Saavedra's "God C..."

S: SurvivalOfConsciousness.com

S: Sukyo Mahikari

"a series of energetic pulses"

We use the same mind-brain system

Our Mind - Body - Spirit (trinity) connects
— Observer   Senses → C
to Source thru the exchange of light energy

* Receive clear perceptions w/out ego distortion. unfiltered by the mind-brain

- Question p. 29.

Ask the ego to stand down.